U N
C O N
V E N
T I O
N A L

SHARON DICKENS

# UN CON VEN TIO NAL

A practical guide

to women's ministry

in the local church

10 Publishing
a division of 10 of those.com

Copyright © 2023 by Sharon Dickens

First published in Great Britain in 2023

British Library Cataloguing in Publication Data
A record for this book is available from the British Library

ISBN: 978-1-914966-75-0

Designed by Jude May
Cover image © Jag_cz | iStock

Printed in Denmark

10Publishing, a division of 10ofthose.com
Unit C, Tomlinson Road, Leyland, PR25 2DY, England

Email: info@10ofthose.com
Website: www.10ofthose.com

1 3 5 7 10 8 6 4 2

# Contents

# Foreword

*Why a Woman Should Be Your First Hire*
Mez McConnell
(Niddrie Community Church, Edinburgh, Scotland)[1]

When I first moved to Niddrie Community Church over 15 years ago, I spent the first six months or so getting to know the then-small congregation. I wanted to find out who was who and who was good at what. I quickly discovered some of the women in the church felt somewhat marginalised and disenfranchised. It appeared they had been left to take a back seat in the life and ministry of the church and in the local community they were trying to reach with the gospel. They were on the usual rotas (tea, coffee and the flowers), but that was about it.

As I began to get to know the community of Niddrie, it became clear to me early on that we needed to hire a community worker, and it needed to be a woman. At that time, complementarianism wasn't as visible as it is now and it was much less common to employ women in churches. Hiring one was a risky move for a new pastor. I had read many articles and blogs by pastors and church planters talking about growing their

---

1. An earlier version of this foreword appeared in Mez McConnell, *The Least, the Last and the Lost*, part IV, chapter 3 (EP, 2021), pp. 375–380.

leadership teams. Very few of them talked about hiring a woman in the early stages of their ministry. Even those that did tended to leave hiring a woman as one of their later appointments and, even then, only if the money came in. I have seen many a planter's development plans, and often women are just not in them. They will talk about hiring a youth worker, an executive pastor or a worship leader before they would even consider a woman.

Churches need to sort out their priorities and make hiring a woman a must. In fact, in our church planting ministry, 20schemes, we insist all our church planters employ a mature woman *from the off* as they embark on their church planting and/or revitalisation venture. Here are some of the reasons why we do that, and why you should do it too.

## Women Make Up a Large Proportion of the Communities We Reach

Whatever church situation you're in, there are going to be a lot of women. Lone parent families make up approximately one quarter of all families living in Scotland in 2019. Unsurprisingly, nine out of ten of these lone parents are women. In the poorest communities in Scotland, 52 per cent of all the residents are women. That is a lot of vulnerable women with multifaceted problems (over half of them suffer from a long-term health problem or a disability). And it'd be a mistake to think that our Scottish context is unique and not mirrored across the western world.

## Women Often Face Multiple Issues Which Complicate Discipleship

Tragically, 45 per cent of women in the UK have experienced at least one incident of interpersonal violence in their lifetime.[2] One in four women have been raped or sexually assaulted as an adult, and five out of every six of those rapes are carried out by someone they know.[3] Other issues like drug abuse and mental health problems affect many women.[4] Many of these vulnerable women with complex physical, psychological, and spiritual problems are in our congregations and are in our communities. Those who have been most hurt often crave love and attention and require a lot of time as we counsel and disciple them in the Word. As their emotional needs are often so great, it's simply wise and prudent for a woman, rather than a man, to invest serious amounts of time into their lives.

## Pastors Are More Likely to Fail Morally If They Get Deeply Involved in Counselling Women

Whilst the statement above is a broad generalisation, a survey of the 15 men who have preceded me at Niddrie Community

---

2. Walby, S. and Allen, J., "Domestic Violence, Sexual Assault and Stalking: Findings from the British Crime Survey", Home Office Research Study 276, March 2004, https://openaccess.city.ac.uk/id/eprint/21697/1/Domesticviolencefindings_2004_5BritishCrimeSurvey276.pdf.

3. https://rapecrisis.org.uk/get-informed/statistics-sexual-violence/

4. Over a quarter of young women aged 16–24 report a common mental health issue in any given week; 40 per cent of people in England who have overlapping problems including homelessness, substance misuse and contact with the criminal justice system have a mental health problem. https://www.mind.org.uk/information-support/types-of-mental-health-problems/statistics-and-facts-about-mental-health/how-common-are-mental-health-problems/

Church revealed one in three of them were removed for offences of sexual immorality. One hundred per cent of these men ran into difficulties through intense counselling with the opposite sex. Sadly, our church leaders are not immune to sexual sin. Many pastors have fallen in this area with a church member they have been counselling or with somebody they have been evangelising. In the schemes where I pastor, counselling and evangelising vulnerable women is a minefield where tenderness or a willingness to listen from a male is almost always misunderstood sexually. Women in deprived areas aren't used to men listening to their problems. They are used to men *being* the problem. But temptation can, for some, be hard to resist in any situation – underprivileged or not. Don't go there.

## Only Women Should Disciple Women

I realise there are many ways pastors can disciple members of their congregation safely, but I suggest having a gifted, trained and mature woman on staff is one of the most helpful ways. In many churches, this type of thing is left to the pastor's wife or maybe the wife of an elder. Almost invariably, this is not because of giftedness but is due to the position her husband holds within the fellowship. It is fine if she is trained, but could be damaging if she is not. Regardless, the point remains that in crisis situations – a daily occurrence here in Niddrie – a mature, godly woman can continue the relationship on into deeper, long-lasting friendship in a way a pastor cannot and should not. When we talk of discipleship, we do not mean the odd monthly pastoral meeting but the intense, daily walk with God as women do life together.

But what is the place for men in this context?

## We Need Godly Men to Teach Women to Train Godly Women

Of course, women need the influence of godly men in their lives. The church is to be led by men after all. That much is clear from Scripture. These men have a responsibility to teach the whole congregation sound doctrine and to model godliness as per Titus 2. But they have a responsibility to teach women too. These are Paul's instructions to Titus:

> *Likewise, teach the older women to be reverent in the way they live, not to be slanderers or addicted to much wine, but to teach what is good. Then they can urge the younger women to love their husbands and children, to be self-controlled and pure, to be busy at home, to be kind, and to be subject to their husbands, so that no one will malign the word of God. (Titus 2:3–5)*

Everything we do at Niddrie Community Church is overseen by the elders and has the approval of the whole congregation. We are clearly involved in the lives of women in our church. Women can see us teach and model godliness in the home and as we preach the Word and lead the meetings. We still counsel couples and single women in certain situations. If I am meeting with a couple, it is with my wife. If meeting with a single woman, it can be with my wife or with one of our women's workers or a friend she trusts. Also, our women's pastoral worker reports to the elders regularly so we can pray intelligently for those with specific needs and difficulties. But, at the heart of it all, we, as the male leaders, are ensuring our women's pastoral workers are being supported and trained to do their job well.

Now, we realise some feel that, by equipping women to pastor and train other women, we are not fulfilling the distinctive male-only role of pastor as we should. Some feel we are confusing people by having women in pastoral positions within the church. When we say our women's worker 'pastors' our women, we don't mean she is a *pastor*; rather, she assists the pastors by providing day-to-day pastoral care to our women. I am often asked by other pastors how we can trust what is being taught and said if we are not present. A few things to say here.

We trust our women because, as with the male leaders, we trained them well in the doctrines of the church before we released them into ministry. It is remarkably offensive to suggest that by giving women responsibility at this level we are opening the church up to serious error. Far more men have led churches astray than women.

The church is not confused but rather is built up as women, and men, are involved in 'one-anothering'. The pastor is not seen as the only one who is qualified to minister among the flock he shepherds. That is a good thing, as one man cannot adequately take on this role. Even with a small church and multiple elders we would struggle under the weight of pastoral issues in our congregation. Women are encouraged that they have a serious part to play in the kingdom of God and that they are not just bystanders or there to cook the meals.

The local church needs women's workers. Most of the women living in our communities are suffering without the hope of the gospel. They have not heard the good news that can set them truly free from their burdens. They need more than someone parachuted in to deal with social problems. They need Christian women to get stuck in to their lives. Women in churches need more than polite small talk and drinks rotas. They need women who will do life with them every single day. The harvest is great, the workers are few, and women are being left on the shelf. They shouldn't be. Employing more women for ministry should be our highest priority.

**Mez McConnell**

Pastor, Niddrie Community Church & Director of 20schemes

# Introduction

I'm standing on the stage talking about my ministry and my experiences as a women's worker from a working-class background. I've done this many times before and I'm always nervous, but this time it's worse. Faces are staring at me, especially from the front row. My eye catches one guy who sits cross-armed, glaring at me with a face that looks like it's been slapped with a wet fish. He's not helping. The clock of doom looms. I'm counting down the minutes left in my talk. I'm intimidated, nervous, fluffing my words. I want to do this important topic justice but I'm dive-bombing. Oh and it's over. Perfect. Straight off the stage, I'm desperate to get out of here. A polite man reminds me I have to stay as I'm part of the panel answering the audience's questions.

Eventually the ordeal is over. I have a one-hour lunch break before the afternoon sessions. As I head off the stage, a queue of people want to ask me questions about women's ministry, training or how to do women's ministry. The queue remains steady for 45 minutes, and, with only 15 minutes of lunch left, the last guy feels sorry for me and says he will email me. I'm high-fiving him in my head; I'm hungry and desperate for a cup of tea.

This isn't something unusual; it happens every time I speak about women's ministry. I would like to tell you it's because

I'm some sort of eloquent and fabulous speaker, but I'm not remotely deluded: it's definitely not me the questioners are interested in but the topic. Church leaders recognise the need for women's ministry but aren't exactly sure how to do it well or even where to start. They have questions about structure, leadership and training. They want to know how to handle specific scenarios or discuss a complex issue with me. In some cases they have tried before to have a women's worker, and it went catastrophically wrong. They have had their fingers burnt, and even though they want to try again, they aren't sure how their elders and congregations would feel a second time around.

It's not just the church leaders who have questions. I come across women who are serving in their communities who feel alone and ill-equipped to deal with the complexity of ministry in poor and deprived areas. The truth is, even though I am writing this book on women's ministry – I can tell you, hand on heart – I feel ill-equipped almost daily. When I see the queue of people after a talk, I always feel out of my depth. I'm usually praying, 'Please. Don't let them ask me a hard question!'

The hardest questions I'm asked are usually from someone who is in terrible pain. The mother of a daughter who is suffering at the hands of an abuser; the woman who is struggling with addiction and afraid to ask for help; the lady who has been hiding a secret for years, afraid the truth will come out. It's heartbreaking. There is little I can do but listen and pray, but it doesn't feel enough. I want to be able to keep in touch and encourage them along the way. I'm always struck by the same thought: *Why aren't they sharing this with someone in their own churches?*

This book is for these very people and their questions: the questions from the church leaders who want to do women's ministry well in a complementarian context; the church member who has been tirelessly serving in a hard area feeling ill-equipped, isolated and unprepared for the task at hand; and the many women who are suffering in silence in our congregations because they feel they can't confide in anyone without judgment or being asked to leave the congregation. This is the reason I agreed to write this book.

## Do We Really Need Another Book About Women's Ministry?

Many of the books about women's ministry give a solid biblical perspective but just stop there – all theory and no application. A biblical description is important, and anyone building a women's ministry needs a solid foundation to build on. But more than this is needed. If the endless books were telling the whole story, then maybe there would not be pastors, church members and women queueing to ask me the same questions over and over again.

When I started over a decade ago, I was, of course, asking the big picture questions, but I also wanted to know how to actually put that into practice on the ground. I wanted examples of how, in a complementarian context, you create good and robust women's ministry that teaches, equips and cares for the women in congregations whilst remaining in submission to the elders. I wanted to read how others built their structure ensuring what was being created didn't become unhinged, independent or unhelpful. What safeguards did they use to ensure what women taught women wasn't fluffy but solid? How do you establish good complementarian women's ministry without becoming egalitarian in disguise? What does accountability really look like? I wanted a how-to guide, my questions answered and someone showing me the pitfalls to avoid. I couldn't find it.

I searched out and read fabulous, well written and absolutely essential books but none of them quite landed the plane where I needed it to. Someone needed to put practical meat on the bones and share examples of what this looks like on the ground. Then I deepened my search and looked for resources that specifically address women's ministry in complex and hard places; it was a barren desert. It was depressing. This is where I hope this book will find its niche.

## What to Expect

*Unconventional* is in all honesty a testimonial of my work in my small evangelical church, Niddrie Community Church (The Mission) in the southeast of Edinburgh, Scotland, and more recently as the Director for Women's Ministry for 20schemes. 20schemes is a ministry which aims to plant 20 gospel-centred churches in the most deprived areas of Scotland and train up the next generation of indigenous leaders. My role involves teaching, training and mentoring women both here in the schemes (housing estates) of Scotland and internationally.

In part 1 of the book, I begin by laying out the theological foundations for a biblical understanding about womanhood and women's ministry. I then share the story of how a women's ministry was developed at Niddrie Community Church. I share a picture of what women's ministry looks like for our church planting ministry, 20schemes, today and map out the journey we took to get here. Building from scratch with no guide was hard. I made mistakes (far too many), God took us in unexpected directions and what we have today doesn't look like the original plan I had in my head.

I will be writing specifically from the perspective of poor, deprived and hard places; after all, this is my context. I'm not suggesting you carbon copy our ministry plan and try to replicate it in your area, because what works in Niddrie, Scotland, won't work in Middlesbrough, England; Kentucky, USA; St. John's, Canada; or Nairobi, Kenya. I am, however, hoping the principles will be transferable in some way. Hopefully, the big issues we wrestled with will help you think through women's ministry in your context. It's with this in mind that throughout this book there will be references to the toolkits in the appendix. These are some of the key toolkits we created for use in our women's ministry training.

In part 2, I will discuss evangelism and discipleship, finishing with the simple, practical application of good accountability and discipleship. It never fails to surprise me when I teach on these topics all over the world just how many people think our discipleship and accountability methods are something new. They aren't, but what they are is well thought-through, strategic and more than the standard Bible study with a little surface application chucked in and no accountability whatsoever. In Niddrie Community Church and 20schemes, robust discipleship and accountability are the foundational bedrock on which we have built the women's ministry. Then finally in part 3, I want to consider some of the key questions and subjects I get asked about.

The voice you hear coming through these pages may be mine, but women's ministry in Niddrie and 20schemes Women isn't a solo effort. We have a team! Our care team at Niddrie

Community Church is made up of wonderful godly women who have quietly and sacrificially served our congregation and its ministries. Without this team and our elders, I would have nothing to say and this book wouldn't exist.

As I write this book I hope some of the truths, principles and resources I highlight will give you a head start and make your life easier as you think through and do women's ministry in your context.

## Further Resources

For more reading on working in deprived areas:

- Sharon Dickens, *Unexceptional: Ordinary Women Doing Extraordinary Things Through God* (10Publishing, 2019)
- Mez McConnell & Mike McKinley, *Church in Hard Places: How the Local Church Brings Life to the Poor and Needy*, 9Marks (Crossway, 2016)

# PART 1

'*Many are the plans in a person's heart, but it is the L*ORD*'s purpose that prevails' (Prov. 19:21).*

# 1

## Different By Design

For over a decade, everywhere I go it feels like the only thing people want to talk about is the role of women in the church. It's always a part of the discussion or one of the questions I'm asked on a panel Q&A. I'm genuinely over this debate. But, as I mentioned in the introduction, if I am going to discuss the practical ins and outs of women's ministry, I must first lay a strong, biblical foundation.

### What is the Role of Women in the Church?

Women have a significant role to play in the life of any church. But exactly what that role is can be an emotive subject for many, causing division and sometimes public debate – which can get quickly messy. Why is this topic so controversial?

First, we must acknowledge there have been – and, in some cases, still are – bad examples in churches of male leadership and complete misuses of power. Sadly, some women (and men) have been spiritually abused, side-lined, unable to serve, treated like lesser humans and oppressed. There have been those who have used Scripture to defend their sinful actions. Let's be clear: Christian feminists weren't protesting without some cause. In fact, 'feminism has drawn attention to a crucial problem that exists for women in society and in the church'.[1] We can't simply brush the ugliness under the table because we don't like it, pretending it wasn't there or didn't happen. Just because that isn't a palatable truth doesn't negate that in some cases it was true.

Second, differences of opinion and scriptural interpretation when it comes to this topic still exist. It's a complete minefield. Even Christians who swim in the same theological pool, so to speak, can disagree on interpretation.

Ultimately, when we start to think about this topic, we must remember not all male leaders abuse their power, not all women hate men and want to rule the world, and not all Christian viewpoints and opinions are biblical. It makes me sad I have to remind us all of that. This topic is complicated, messy and confusing. So where do we start? How can we possibly navigate this subject, avoiding the potholes and distractions, and start to explore it well?

In one chapter we aren't going to have time to delve into the biblical minutia or cultural context for the text or even debate the interpretation of just one significant word. But I do want to give a brief overview and recommend some helpful resources for further study (this is an important topic, so I hope you will study it further!).

I want to specifically look at the impact of recent history, the three primary Christian views and the elder/pastor headship role.

---

1. Mary Kassian, *The Feminist Mistake: The Radical Impact of Feminism on Church and Culture* (Crossway, 2005), p. 10.

## Impact of Recent History

As long as I can remember, I have known about the importance of the women's vote and the price that was paid to make sure I had a voice in the political arena. I cannot remember one specific moment or conversation, but I have no doubt my mother was very influential in planting this seed.

It would be so easy for us to think originally feminism was just about the right to vote, but it was about so much more. In the UK, and eventually the US, it focused on the promotion of equal contracts, marriages, parenting rights, child custody, education and property rights for women.

Feminism started in the late 1700s with a publication written by Mary Wollstonecraft called *A Vindication of the Rights of Woman*. The late 1800s and early 1900s started to see real traction for feminism, with changes to the law and legislation being adopted in the Western world. Legal, political, economic and educational barriers that had been restricting women were slowly being demolished – barriers we still see in many parts of the world today. As Western troops withdrew from Afghanistan in 2021, women in key roles had to leave, go into hiding or step down. We watched as images of women were painted over, slowly disappearing. We have been moved by, affected by and horrified by these types of injustices. Few Christians would question us praying about and even protesting these wrongs.

Subsequent waves of feminism have been different. They haven't only looked at the existing inequality (fewer rights, less pay for the same job, treatment as the 'second/lesser sex', limited education, domestic violence, marital rape and so on). Quickly the primary focus became women's happiness. Women were seen to be discontent, dissatisfied, frustrated and straitjacketed by a lack of fulfilment. The assumption was that *all* women were dissatisfied and confined within their 'enforced' roles.

Within the church, women vocalised their discontent against the different treatment they received. Author and speaker Mary Kassian explains the development of feminism in the church: 'Christian feminists began to pursue the inclusion of women in leadership hierarchies without a clear analysis of whether or not the hierarchies themselves were structured and functioning according to a biblical pattern.'[2] Christian feminists argued that women's exclusion from leadership may have had some validity at one point, but that this was a cultural and historical practice, and as times had changed, so this should too.

Christian feminists started to reject a theology that they felt had its roots in patriarchy. They questioned all aspects of theology and doctrine. I would suggest *Christian feminists allowed their worldview to affect how they interpreted the Bible instead of allowing the Bible to affect how they interpreted the world*. I feel like I should pause and underline that a few hundred times or write it in flashy lights. The fundamental lie at the heart of Christian feminism is simply this: it claims to give us something that God has already pre-designed and established clearly in his Word – equality. Men and women are created equal in his image.

Writer Claire Smith goes even further, suggesting in Christian feminism, 'it was not equality with men that was sought but a reversal of order so that women would rule where men once did'.[3] Feminism, notes Smith, has 'brought huge and radical

2. Mary Kassian, *The Feminist Mistake*, p. 32.
3. Claire Smith, *God's Good Design: What the Bible Really Says about Men and Women* (Matthias Media, 2012), p. 14.

cultural changes. It is difficult to think of any element of society or our lives that has been immune from it'.[4] Again, Smith puts it like this: the 'dust of feminism has settled on the pages of our Bibles and obscured God's word...feminism has reached into every corner of Christian truth. Even God has had a feminist makeover.'[5] Smith describes it like the fine red dust, after builders have been working, that settles all over the house and takes endless cleaning to get rid of. It's so fine, it gets into every nook and cranny, even in the most inaccessible and unreachable areas. This is why I'm belabouring the point – feminism is so fine a dust many of us don't even realise we are being influenced by it. I would suggest some of the discussions started by second-wave feminism and the focus on sexuality opened the door for much of the thinking and ambiguity we have around sexual identity today. But that's a discussion for another day.

We need to be honest about what's influencing us as we think through the topic of the role of women in the church.

## Three Primary Christian Views

As we shift into a brief definition of the three primary views it's worth saying that even within each definition, some people will be far more fundamental whilst others will be more liberal in certain areas. After all, we all have our own biblical interpretations, contextual influences, emotional narratives and agendas that influence us as we come to the discussion.

So, how do you know what's true and what to believe? I would simply repeat what I said earlier: Don't allow your worldview

---

4. Ibid. p. 12.
5. Ibid. p. 12.

to affect how you interpret the Bible. Instead allow the Bible to affect and impact how you interpret the world.

Here is my attempt at simple definitions for the three Christian views.

### Egalitarian

*Egalitarian* means men and women are partners together in every aspect of ministry and life. All ministries and offices in the church are open to all qualified church members – men and women. Gender should not and does not exclude any person from any church office, including the office of elder, pastor or minister.

### Complementarian

*Complementarian* means men and women are absolutely equal but have been created for different roles which complement each other. Claire Smith notes, 'One of the fallacies of much feminist ideology is the belief that for two people to be equal, they must do the same thing. There is an assumption that you cannot have differentiation and order without also having inferiority and superiority of dignity or worth.'[6] For complementarians, all church ministries are open to qualified men and women with the exception of elder and pastor, which is only open to qualified men. Women can serve in many roles and even be in full-time paid ministry.

We see this pattern in the Trinity, all equally divine yet with different roles: 'All the three persons of the Godhead share in the same divine being and nature, yet there is an asymmetry within the divine relationships. There is sameness and equality alongside functional or relational order. It is not a case of either equality or order, but both equality and sameness, and order and difference.'[7]

---

6. Ibid. p. 63.
7. Ibid. p. 63.

There are a few clear distinctions in the roles of men and women within the church, but there are also significant corresponding ways men and women are called and equipped by God to participate in the ministry of the local church and the work of the gospel. We aren't just allowed, but expected, to participate in the ministry and practices of our local church. We have been saved for a purpose after all.

I would suggest complementarian is the true biblical interpretation of God's Word. This viewpoint influences what I'm saying in this book.

### Hierarchical

Hierarchical means women and men are created to operate in different areas of church ministry. Women cannot serve as elders or deacons, serve communion, teach men, lead worship or speak in the church service. Women can only build ministries for women and children. There are those who even go as far as questioning whether women can write Bible commentaries or be in leadership roles of any kind, such as being a prime minister or even a member of parliament.

### What Being Complementarian Is Not

There's an awful lot of confusion out there about being complementarian. It's important to understand what being complementarian is not.

*Complementarian is not spiritually abusive.* I have sadly heard the opposite of this statement many times, and there are some who believe complementarian theology leaves women open to abuse. Let me be very clear: it's not God's Word that's abusive. Sadly, the horrifying truth is sometimes a sinful church leader is abusive, ungodly and bang out of order. Abusers can and do misuse Scripture to back up their sinful behaviour. If you are reading this and you are a woman who has been badly hurt, oppressed and abused by a man in authority who wielded his manipulative interpretation of God's Word as an excuse for his oppression and abuse toward you, then I am so sorry you have been hurt in such a horrific and evil way. It's wrong. We need to call this sin out. It is not the caring, compassionate, loving leadership we see exampled in Christ.

*Complementarian is not being a closet egalitarian.* I remember a conversation with a lady who said she was complementarian, but in truth she was really a closet egalitarian. What she said simply didn't pan out in her life. The topic being debated was 'Can a woman teach (preach) on a Sunday in a mixed setting (to both men and women) if there is an elder present?' Her argument was that when she taught she was under spiritual authority because the elder was present. *Sigh.* The debate will melt your head as you try to define the different versions of speaking, teaching and preaching. The Bible is much clearer. Kevin DeYoung puts it like this: 'The heraldic event – no matter the platform provided by the pastor or the covering given by the elders – cannot be separated from exercising authority and teaching, the two things women are not permitted to do in the worship service.'[8]

*Complementarian does not undermine women's gifts.* One of the arguments I hear a lot in favour of women pastors is 'Why would God give a woman a gift for teaching if he didn't expect

---

8. Kevin DeYoung, 'Should Women Preach in Our Churches?', The Gospel Coalition, 26 August 2019, https://www.thegospelcoalition.org/blogs/kevin-deyoung/women-preach-churches/

her to use it?' I don't deny women can have a gift for teaching the Word, but I would argue about *how* we are to use that God-given gift. There are many opportunities in an active congregation for church members to embrace *all* their gifts, even those with a gift of teaching. The same is true for the men in the congregation who are gifted teachers but not able to exercise that from the pulpit.

The Bible is very clear: the public, authoritative proclamation of God's Word, the preaching of the sermon, is not open to women – they shouldn't teach in a mixed setting. We can debate until the cows come home the interpretation of verses that say women are not permitted to teach men or have authority over them, but it does not change the reality of the biblical truth. Arguments aiming to limit or change the distinction of this text don't hold water. We can't simply say it's not for today. Biblical authors aren't just challenging or addressing a local cultural issue; there is a consistent and theological pattern found throughout Scripture. 1 Timothy 2 is clear – women are not to have authority over men in the Christian gathering. Whatever your gift set is from God, he would expect that gift to be used and exercised biblically.

## The Elder/Pastor Headship Role

*Now the overseer is to be above reproach, faithful to his wife, temperate, self-controlled, respectable, hospitable, able to teach, not given to drunkenness, not violent but gentle, not quarrelsome, not a lover of money. He must manage his own family well and see that his children obey him, and he must do so in a manner worthy of full respect. (If anyone does not know how to manage*

*his own family, how can he take care of God's church?) He must*
*not be a recent convert, or he may become conceited and fall*
*under the same judgment as the devil. He must also have a good*
*reputation with outsiders, so that he will not fall into disgrace and*
*into the devil's trap. (1 Timothy 3:2–7)*

It's no mistake Paul discussed the key roles of men and women
in the church just before he gets to the qualifications for elder/
pastor roles. He stated women aren't permitted to teach men or
exercise authority over the church. Paul lays the foundational
groundwork, and then in 1 Timothy 3:2–7 he simply launches
into the qualifications for male shepherds to oversee the body
of Christ, and it is quite the list. To me, this is obvious (but then
I'm a simple soul who likes to stick to the text): the overseer/
elder/shepherd equals a man (a 'he'). It's a role only open to
qualified men.

By looking at the relational pattern of headship we see in this
text – but also throughout the whole of Scripture and ultimately
modelled within the Trinity – we can't deny a pattern exists, even
if we would want to. Scripture consistently tells the same story
and follows the same pattern for a reason, and we are supposed
to take note.

## Relationship Patterns

We see the same relational pattern in 1 Corinthians 11:3: 'But I
want you to understand that the head of every man is Christ, the
head of a wife is her husband, and the head of Christ is God' (ESV).

*In this verse, Paul is using the word 'head' to talk about order and*
*authority in relationships. So, this verse tells us something about*

*the relationship of the Trinity, which provided the context for Paul's instruction for men and women. It tells us there is order within the Godhead, and the persons of the Trinity (at least the first two) relate in some sort of hierarchical relationship.*[9]

We see this relational pattern, for example, played out in the creation order as God creates humankind which is male and female:

*Genesis does not gesture toward the generic plurality of humanity. Instead, humanity's maleness and femaleness renders us a race and establishes the primary bonds of our natural relations and the source of our given identities... [In Genesis 3] a gendered differentiation becomes more explicit, not least in the fact that the priestly task chiefly falls to the man, rather than his wife.*[10]

Think it through with me and hear me out. Consider, for example, the relationship between men and women in marriage: it reflects the relationships of the Trinity where God the Father has headship over God the Son and God the Holy Spirit. If God is so concerned that marriage reflects this relational order, then it makes no sense to me that when it comes to the church (Christ's bride) the patterns would suddenly change. God intends the same relationship order to play out in the body of Christ, his church. This relational order is beyond cultural impacts; it's foundationally eternal. Even the texts outlining

9. Claire Smith, *God's Good Design*, p. 62–3.
10. Alastair Roberts, 'Man and Woman in Creation (Genesis 1 and 2)', 9Marks.org, 12 October 2019, https://www.9marks.org/article/man-and-woman-in-creation-genesis-1-and-2/

the qualifications for an elder refer to the playing out of the relationship pattern dynamic. According to 1 Timothy 3:5, elders need to lead, oversee and teach their families well: 'If anyone does not know how to manage his own family, how can he take care of God's church?'. Elders have an extraordinary responsibility and will be held to account before God for how they have taught, shepherded and protected the church (Jas. 3:1). Knowing a little of the pastoral situations our elders have to contend with, I'm thankful for the men God has given us and selfishly grateful it's not my responsibility and never will be as a woman.

I suspect the endless debate will forever continue around this subject, but I'll only be wading in when I'm forced to. Scripture is clear and attested to by the creational order and the relational Godhead: no matter the cultural context, the overseer/elder/shepherd is a role only open to qualified men. We can't simply brush truth aside and cast it off as tradition. It's how God intended it to be.

## Further Resources

- Ligon Duncan & Susan Hunt, *Women's Ministry in the Local Church* (Crossway, 2006)
- Gloria Furman & Kathleen Nielson, *Word-Filled Women's Ministry: Loving and Serving the Church* (Crossway, 1st Ed., 2015)
- Bobby Jamieson, *Leading One Another: Church Leadership*, 9Marks Healthy Church Study Guides (Crossway, 2012)
- Claire Smith, *God's Good Design: What the Bible Really Says about Men and Women* (Matthias Media, 2012)

# 2

## Understanding the Past and Present

**The Past**

I have been at Niddrie Community Church for a long time, years before our pastor Mez McConnell arrived and offered me a job. This usually surprises people. Even though I felt part of the church family, I found church difficult to navigate (a square peg trying to fit in a round hole, I always said). There never really seemed to be any clear role for me to do besides the tea rota and youth work. I'm not the best at making tea, but I did take part in the youth work for years, bringing my mum tone and my kids along with me. I used to talk to my friend who was a minister, and he would say, 'Leave your church, and come to us. I have loads of work you can be doing.' It was tempting, but I knew without a shadow of a doubt I was supposed to be at Niddrie and learn whatever lesson I was supposed to.

On the Scottish Government's deprivation index, Niddrie, the scheme (housing estate) I live in, is ranked as the most deprived in Edinburgh. I could fill your head with all sorts of statistics and data, but the truth is this would paint a very one-sided picture of what Niddrie is like, and that picture would be a very stark and sad one.

Niddrie has serious crime, health and drug problems, but there are also some really caring people who are hard-working, fiercely loyal and protective. There is a real creative art culture going on, especially in music (check out 20schemes Music). The truth is, there is good and bad, and most of the time it's twisted into one melting pot. It's fair to say life in my community is hard for many. Not because it's a hard place to share the gospel (it's sympathetic to the supernatural, and people still believe God exists), but it's hard because life in Niddrie is just hard. Life expectancy is lower than nearby wealthier areas, and they don't die young because life is a bed of roses. It's soul-destroying seeing yet another die without salvation, without the hope of the gospel.

I don't know how to describe our church in the 1990s and early 2000s. As a congregation we ran a community café, but felt we had to bring in people from other churches to man it; they were like polite, non-scary bouncers. I remember a scheme girl once blagged her way into the kitchen, and she was set to work straight away taking the money – until she got caught stealing. Others were openly dealing in the café, and the volunteers didn't even notice. Nice, lovely, kind and gracious Christians but inexperienced in dealing with the Niddrie community.

As a congregation, I would say we were well-meaning but never really managed to engage particularly well with the community. Looking back, we clearly deluded ourselves into thinking we were making great strides. The youth clubs were a constant battle and the church building was being systematically vandalised and attacked – at times it felt a little like we were under siege. My favourite was when they glued the locks, and we couldn't get in the building for the Sunday service. We had the service in the grassy area a couple of minutes from church that day. Sadly, not all the harassment was prank style, as church members were harassed, windows smashed, car tyres slashed or vehicles totalled and set on fire. The congregation were seriously godly people who loved the Lord. But, in the main, we didn't have a scooby about the place we were serving.

When our pastor Mez arrived in 2007, things didn't change straight away and the hassles didn't suddenly stop. But change did happen. The dealers were slung out the door sharpish, and the community police came on a regular basis. One massive and completely necessary change did happen overnight: the church policy changed on volunteering so only members of the Niddrie Community Church committed to the area could serve. Our elders challenged us to get to know, live in, and actively be a part of the Niddrie community.

Mez arrived in September and started talking to me about working at the church in October. Honestly, I was surprised at first. I always suspected he had been pre-warned about certain 'problem women' in our church, and I'm fairly certain I was at the top of that list. Square peg, round hole, remember. I'm not a middle-class, churched girlie, but a scheme girl with aspirations!

Now you need to understand three things here. First, it was not an exciting employment package I was being offered. Mez basically said, 'Come work for me. I can't pay you anything yet, but God will sort it out.' The thought wasn't enticing; I was a single parent and my two kids' sole provider.

Second, I was fearful. I mean seriously boat-tossed-by-the-waves on a daily basis, terrified to step out in faith. I would have been different without my children, but I was scared for them. I knew skint; we had had no money for bread and milk before, and I didn't want to be there again.

From the first discussion to the point of employment was a six-month roller-coaster of fear and doubt. Eventually, when I got over myself, repented and trusted God, Mez proposed our congregation employ me for one year as a community worker. Surprisingly, they agreed, and within one weekend they had pledged enough money to pay me. In April 2008, I left my secure job behind without a backward glance, accepting the drop in salary as the journey began. I would like to tell you I was full of confidence and faith, but I'm a weak and feeble sinner; it took me a long time to fully trust God.

Third, Mez received some serious flack for employing me (not only from within our fellowship but from other Christian leaders also). I was a female, divorced and the single parent of two kids. I could almost hear people's thoughts, 'Think of the example she might be setting!' Mez was amazing at protecting me from most of that, but occasionally someone felt *compelled* to share their opinion with me personally. Occasionally, they still feel compelled.

I wanted to share a bit about how this journey began for two main reasons. First, everyone seems to have this crazy ideal of what the perfect women's worker looks like. But in real life, the perfect women's worker for your church might be some proper random (like me) who is sitting in the pew waiting to be offered the chance to fly. I know a feisty, loud, strong-minded single parent who was divorced and carrying a trunkload of baggage doesn't seem like the ideal candidate for a women's worker. I agreed. Even I would have suggested someone else. Truthfully, it has taken me over a decade to realise the DNA of our women's ministry at Niddrie and our subsequent church planting ministry, 20schemes, would have looked completely different with someone else driving it forward. Hear me well: I don't think I'm the 'perfect' women's worker (I want to dispel the myth that there is such a thing as that), but I am who God chose for the job.

Second, it is far too easy to look at Niddrie and 20schemes now, with what we have in place, and think we have it all together. We didn't wake up one morning and have it all sewn up and sorted. We weren't a big mega-church with endless money and reams of resources. We were just 44 members, a building and a vision.

## The Present
### Niddrie Community Church (NCC)

At NCC I am on a care team with eight other wonderful women – four of us have been on the team from the beginning. Our women's coordinator, Natasha Davidson, organises us and is the connection to our elders, reporting to them on a monthly basis. As church members we all have access to the elders anytime we need to, but our first port of call, as a care team, is Natasha. As a group, we meet on a monthly basis for fellowship, prayer and to deal with any concerns.

These eight women are amazing. With a congregation of around 120 people on a Sunday, and probably double that number in community contacts, no matter how good we are or how much time we have, we simply can't be intentional and disciple every woman on our own.

We each have one or two women we see on a one-to-one basis and encourage them to see someone else one-to-one also. Around 90 per cent of our female church members have a one-to-one. I'm going to visit this relationship later in this book, but, in brief, a one-to-one discipleship relationship is between two female church members and is based on the pattern of Titus 2. It is a more mature Christian discipling a younger woman, helping her grow in the faith and learn what it means to be a godly woman. This relationship is intentional, not distant or perfunctory. It's way more than a weekly Bible study, a quick coffee and a prayer. One-to-one relationships are life-on-life, committed, sometimes 24/7, warts and all, and can be messy and scary.

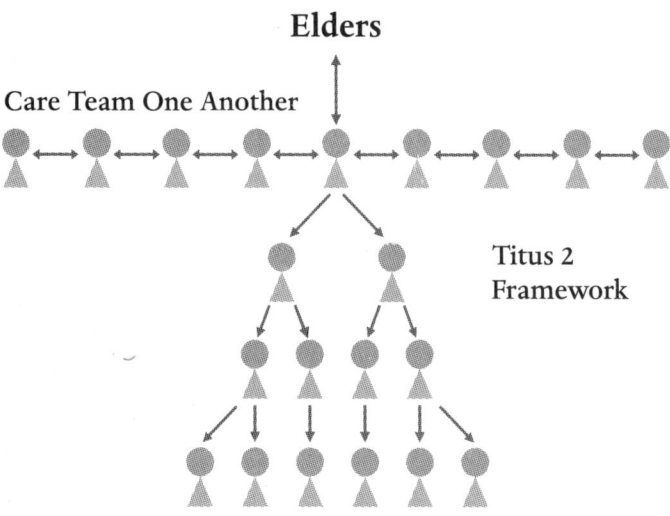

Example of a Titus 2 framework and the impact of one member

We have a thought-out plan for a discipleship pathway. This plan is from point zero to maturity and includes, among other things, the books, the resources and the way to encourage gifts and service.

We have a book list which is useful for new believers, people grieving, those struggling with singleness and so on. Our ladies can pick any book or resource from the list and be assured it's solid and biblical and not fluff. Anyone can suggest a new book to be added, but all resources and teaching material we use (even what we write ourselves) first must be approved by an elder. Now, I know you might be sitting there thinking that's a tad overbearing and harsh, but I would challenge that. It's loving and caring. Our elders are providing essential biblical quality control and leadership. As parents, we wouldn't hand our kids any old book or video game to engage with before we ensured it was good, sensible, age-appropriate and helpful. Yet, with young Christians, far too often they are reading unhelpful and unbiblical Christian fluff that isn't remotely good for their growth and souls. Sadly, this is true for many older Christians also.

The NCC's pathway gives our ladies who lead one-to-ones a road map for discipleship, ensuring they have guidance and help.

One important thing to note. When I travel and visit churches, much of the women's ministry I see is events driven: Bible studies, teaching events or craft fairs.

Although we do have events at NCC, it's not the driving force of our ministry. The foundation of our women's ministry is our one-to-one discipleship relationships. This approach changed the dynamic of everything we do.

### 20schemes

I have been on staff at Niddrie Community Church for well over a decade, primarily in the role of women's coordinator. In 2017, my elders asked me to change my focus and serve primarily with our church-planting ministry, 20schemes. This wasn't an easy transition as I love the buzz and the banter of serving the community. Thankfully, I remain on the women's care team at church, so I'm no longer coordinating that work but still involved.

My new role at 20schemes is wider, encompassing the whole of Scotland. In a nutshell, I was asked to continue working with women, taking the lessons learnt at Niddrie and in some way create a ministry that trains, mentors and disciples women and the ministry wives connected to 20schemes church plants. This ministry has grown beyond Scotland as we train internationally and care for women in similar roles and contexts through our 20schemes' Women's Network.

At 20schemes my main focus is developing the women's ministry and training and mentoring women's workers. Miriam McConnell and Lorne Millar are also on my team. Miriam's role is to mentor and care for 20schemes' church planters' wives. Lorne is basically my right-hand girl dealing with the day-to-day administration of our ministry. To be honest, we follow the very similar Titus 2 framework: more mature and experienced women speaking into the lives of other women. The key difference with 20schemes is we do not undertake one-to-one accountability relationships with women outside of NCC on a long-term basis. The one-to-one accountability relationship needs to be established with someone from their church plant.

It has been much harder to ensure we don't become simply an events provider at 20schemes Women. As with the discipleship relationships at NCC, we have worked hard to ensure the mentoring relationship with the women's worker or ministry wife is at the centre of all that we do. Our role is to train, prepare and equip them to serve their church plants more effectively.

Here is an overview of the different resources and training opportunities we have at 20schemes:

*Discipleship.* 20schemes Women will disciple the main women's workers for the first year of their training. This ensures that we pass on the accountability DNA before one-to-one relationships are taken on by church plants locally.

*Mentoring.* We provide continual mentoring, evaluation and training of all key women's workers and ministry wives.

*Women's Fraternal.* This is a monthly training session for women who are more actively serving their church plants. We teach our interns and others more about the Bible and how they can teach the Bible to others. This is about more than teaching and training; it's an opportunity to fellowship, pray and support each other. Quarterly we split into smaller groups.

*20schemes Women Pre-Conference.* Twice a year we hold a women's pre-conference with three keynote speakers on a variety of topics.

*Ragged Women Ministry Elective.* At the Ragged School of Theology we deliver a Women's Ministry Certificate as well as a Ministry Wives' Induction. Both of these classes can be taken remotely.

*20schemes Equip Training.* We have developed a number of online training courses, which can be found at 20schemesequip. org, such as the Titus 2 Women course, which is available to any church member who wants to think through how she can be more intentional and effective in her context.

*20schemes Women Resources*. We strive to develop and produce resources such as books and training programmes to further the work.

Developing the training was seriously difficult in the beginning, cobbling bits of this and a section of that to make something work for us. I remember how labour-intensive and frankly demoralising that was. In the end, we started building our programme from scratch and created our own.

The end of this chapter may have felt a little bit like an advertisement for what we do, but that was not my intention. Please don't think I'm trying to brag somehow, saying, 'Look how amazing we are.' Far from it. I would actually love it if you look at the list and say, 'They have done the heavy lifting, so I just need to make it work in my context. I can focus my limited time on the people around me.' The best place to start is our monthly news and prayer letter. This is where you will get a flavour of what we do, and often we send out downloads of pre-conference sessions to listen to for free. To receive it, please email admin@20schemes.com.

# 3

## Beginning of a Ministry

I had been in my role as Community Development Worker at Niddrie Community Church (NCC) for six months when I said to my pastor Mez, 'This is a job for two people!' I was talking about running the community café full time while also organising the women's ministry in the community and church. He laughed and said, 'I know.' But then he asked an interesting question: 'Which role do you think is yours?' I didn't even have to think for more than a millisecond before replying I thought it was the café. I didn't particularly find his response helpful as, laughing, he told me to go away and think about it and come back when I had changed my mind. 'You need to get a vision for women's ministry,' was his parting shot.

To be honest, I had not really thought about women's ministry; I didn't even know what it was, and clearly it wasn't what I had envisaged my role would be. I saw myself bashing around the community café, sharing the gospel while chucking the banter around with everyone who came through the door, and things like that. I mean, how could one miraculously whip up a vision for women's work? What did I know about women's ministry? I didn't even know if I wanted to do it. So, I prayed.

I had been a member of many churches over my 30-plus years of faith, but, when I thought back, I had never been anywhere where there had been an active women's ministry. There were always pockets of women meeting *ad hoc*, but nothing formal or structured. So, what did women's ministry look like? I started contacting other churches to see what they offered, but drew a blank. They did not have a women's ministry or women's worker. Not one. I had never noticed this before. Eventually I came across one part-time female pastoral worker, working for a city-centre church. Her role was mostly pastoral visiting. Was this women's ministry? Maybe in some small way. But there had to be more to it than visiting the older members of the church. I couldn't really see myself just visiting people, having tea and cake, sharing a quick bit of Scripture and saying a wee prayer. The women I spent time with needed more.

In time our pastor's wife Miriam took over my role in the café as I changed my role to women's coordinator, and I knew it was the right move. Next question to tackle was where to start. There was no template out there or examples of what I thought would be helpful or would work in our context. I was supposed to come up with a plan for our elders. My plan needed to outline the vision I had for women's ministry, how it would work and how I planned to implement that.

### 'You Need to Think About Titus 2'

Mez has an infuriating habit of being unhelpfully helpful. He tends to drop these little thought-bombs into conversation and then leave you to mull it over. He said to me once, 'You need to think about Titus 2.' Then in a staff meeting a few days later he handed us all a sheet of paper and told us he wanted us to be accountable to one another, making it clear Miriam and I would meet weekly with each other for this purpose (we call this one-anothering these days – an equal relationship of discipling each other). As I looked at the paper, I saw the 10 questions he wanted us to go through, and I thought, 'Are you being serious? I'm not telling the pastor's wife anything!' It was strange at first, but we got over ourselves eventually. In reality I would say it took me and Miriam about two years to get to the point where we could have a no-holds-barred conversation. I also started asking the female members of the congregation if they wanted to have an accountability relationship with me or Miriam. Surprisingly, most said yes.

Accountability was just a small part of the women's ministry. On the surface it looked like we were doing great things, like meeting with the congregation and being intentional with the women in the community. It was busy. There was a lot to do, and, although Miriam was working part time, there was no way we could do everything on our own. There were too many people and not enough time or staff to help. Thankfully, Mez threw in another one of his thought-bombs, 'You need to think about a team.'

A team? How would that work? What would they do? How could I persuade them to come and help? Who would I ask? How would I train them?

## An Honest Review

With these questions and more running around my head, it was time to take an honest look at our existing women's ministry.

How on earth can you review something that doesn't really exist? In the end, I made a list of everything going on at church that could remotely be classified as women's ministry. Then I asked some really hard questions and faced the reality of how they functioned and what they were accomplishing.

Here are eight questions you can ask of your church's women's ministry:

1. What is the aim and purpose of the ministry?
2. Who is it serving?
3. Does it really meet those needs?
4. Who attends? Non-believers, members, etc.
5. What are the strengths and weaknesses?
6. Do we need to close it down or reinvent it?
7. What changes are needed?
8. How are we going to make those changes happen?

In the cold light of day, it was hard reviewing ministries people loved and that had been in existence for decades. Sometimes I wonder if we do things just because they are habits that became part of the church culture but aren't needed today. For the review to be effective it had to be honest – seriously considering every ministry in light of the gospel and the church mission statement – and it could not be influenced by my fear of man. The hardest thing was to admit a ministry simply wasn't working, had served its purpose and had to close.

One such ministry was the women's meeting. The meeting had been running at NCC for years. A few times, I had even been the speaker. Every Tuesday afternoon, five women and one man would come to the women's meeting, they would have tea and cake, sing a few old-school hymns and listen to a 20-minute message. What was so bad about that? I had to work through the eight questions above honestly for the women's meeting, no matter how much I struggled with the answers.

Here's what I found: (1) The main aim of the women's meeting was clear: to serve the female members of NCC and to share the gospel. (2) Serving the older generation of NCC and other churches, the group was a social time of fellowship and friendship for the older saints. (3) However, it clearly wasn't evangelistic and we couldn't have invited our new contacts to this wee group. (4) Also, only three of the women attending came from NCC; the other ladies travelled in from other churches in the city.

(5) I could see the strengths: these women loved the Lord and a few were great at getting alongside the young mums with toddlers in a sort of beloved-old-aunt role. However, the weaknesses were evident. They had an older gentleman in the group, and although I understood why he wanted to come, it created practical issues as women were clearly teaching in a mixed setting. Many were stuck in their ways and didn't want anything to change. The ladies who were not part of NCC didn't really want to engage with a community they weren't part of.

(6) To close or not? This was one of the hardest questions to grapple with. The lady running the group wanted to step down and expected me to take over, and it was increasingly difficult to find speakers every week. I really adored the woman who was leading and I didn't want to hurt her, but I knew the meeting had to close. (7) Meanwhile we had a growing group of older people coming into the café who were starting to feel welcome. Niddrie has a community of older people who were

perhaps isolated and lonely, and we needed to engage with them, sharing the gospel in a more focused and intentional way. (8) And so, it became clear we needed to close the women's meeting and launch an over-50s group. We needed to bring all the ladies from the women's meeting and the wider church members along to befriend and engage with the community and tell them about Jesus.

It was hard to systematically go through each ministry reflecting and reviewing what was really going on. Asking the hard questions, however, did enable me to see what was *really* happening, and not just what I *thought* was happening. With a few tweaks and refocusing, many of the ministries could be more effective; others would need to come to an end.

One of the key issues about evaluating the existing women's ministry at NCC was simply that it didn't really exist in any structured or strategical form. What could be loosely defined as women's ministry was informal and unsupervised. This is not to suggest what was going on was not done well; merely, it was conducted without accountability and oversight. There was no imbedded structure or benchmark, so to speak. How could the elders be sure this ministry was appropriate and conducted with biblical integrity? I wasn't alone in my presuppositions that everyone in my church was mature or biblically astute, but it simply wasn't true. Much of the interaction with women was informal, and it was at times difficult to consider how well these women were speaking into each other's lives.

I had a lot of questions and much to think about. The review, my questions and my conclusions became the foundations of my women's ministry plan for the elders. Nothing could move forward without their approval and help.

## Extract From the First Ministry Plan

I want to share with you a brief extract from the first draft of the plan, which went through a number of revisions, re-evaulations and lessons learnt from mistakes on the ground, before it became the finished article. From the outset, I wanted to establish a team who had the ability to pastorally care for others in the membership and, to some extent, non-members. I proposed creating a training plan for the care team and an accountability structure to ensure they cared for each other well, meeting monthly as a group and monthly with their accountability partner.

I envisaged three levels of care in the original plan:

- Level 1 – One-to-One:
  - o Evangelistic relationship building: We would build relationships with women in the community. Members have had some difficulties interacting with the community on a meaningful level. To combat this, the strategic plan is to slowly introduce women from the membership into existing established community relationships and nurture them for a while, bridging the gap and encouraging useful conversation between the women.
  - o Discipleship mentoring for non-members: We will have a one-to-one beginner's study and accountability with ample support. The mature Christian will be the one person the new believer talks to instead of needing to go to many others. The mentoring will include Bible exploration using the approved literature.

- o  Members action: There are many women in the congregation who lack maturity or integrity, who may simply need a mentor to help them in the 'weaning' process as they step into maturity. We propose a one-to-one Bible study working through an agreed series of approved books.
- Level 2 – Small Group Work: Periodic short-term Bible studies tackling various issues prominent in the lives of the women we care for. These meetings will be open to any women in the community or church who want to come.
- Level 3 – Communal Care: We would hold conference Saturday afternoons (with lunch), which would be a time of teaching, worship, fellowship, prayer and group session work.

This skeleton should be enough to paint a picture. In your context, the review would be different. What works for you wouldn't work for us in Niddrie. But, as with any review, you need to understand several things: the ministry, the context and the culture.

I can't stress how important it is to really understand the culture and context well. Let me give you a simple example. In our schemes it's not culturally normal for adults to have dinner at their friend's house. If your children have their friends over and it's dinner time, they often stay for the evening meal. Adult friends won't. No dinner parties, thank you. But we do nip in and out for a cup of tea.

In the early days, one of our new indigenous believers asked me, 'Shabba, are all these people asking me to their house for dinner to test if I'll steal from them?' Something so small and seemingly insignificant can be so important. Another time one of our male workers asked a guy in the café whom he had been chatting with to come to his house for tea. The invite didn't go down well and Mez had to step in and stop the guy threatening the worker. Why would the worker's invite be weird? Context and culture are key: the guy thought he was being sexually propositioned and didn't take kindly to the idea. We must understand the nuances of our context and culture.

At that time, on a Sunday at NCC, our dominant culture was Christian and middle-class. However, new believers were unchurched and predominantly on benefits or had working-class backgrounds. Cue a massive culture clash. Any ministry plan must reflect the cultural dynamics that exist in your context. To do any review justice you must understand all the dynamics at play. Sometimes the dominant culture isn't the most helpful or reliable for bringing about change.

## Appendix Toolkit

- Appendix 1: Women's Ministry Plan Outline

# 4

# The Care Team

**Choosing a Care Team**

The obvious place to start building a care team would be to find the most pastorally gifted and teachable women in the congregation. I know it seems obvious, but unless she is an active and accountable church member, then no matter how gifted she may be, give her a wide berth. There is no accountability or discipline if something goes wrong unless the team is made up of church members subject to the authority of the elders. I can't stress it enough: if she can't or won't commit to the responsibility of being a member, she is not the person you are looking for (no matter how gifted she is).

While thinking of the women who could be on the care team, I didn't want to pick just the usual suspects. Looking beyond the obvious was important to me. As with many churches, we had women who came to everything and always served no matter the task. Lovely, servant-hearted women, but I knew some weren't gifted pastorally. I was intentional, watching how women interacted with each other. Did they spend each Sunday talking with the same faces, or did they make an effort with the more vulnerable, the older ladies, the ones on the fringes or the ladies from the schemes? I wanted to know what kind of advice they gave. Were they afraid to tell others hard truths, did they spout fluff or did they just say what others wanted to hear? I paid attention to how people responded to the struggles in life. This is not as hard a task as you may think if you pay attention and are involved first-hand in the lives of women. I was searching for the women in our congregation who were teachable and mature and who had a pastoral gift.

My list was coming together. Some were, of course, the obvious choices, but others were much more unexpected. It's fascinating to look back on my first list before I had really thought it through or actively sought a care team. I had been guessing and filling in names just because I figured they would be good at it without actually reflecting properly. There were women I had imagined would be amazing but, on further examination and thought, didn't really have the appropriate gift set. They were all godly women with a heart to serve, but, looking back, some weren't as mature as I thought they were (old doesn't necessarily equate to Christian maturity). If I had gone with that first imaginary list and hadn't really been intentional, honestly, I think the women's ministry would have completely bombed. So, as you build your care team, do your homework and take your time. Make sure you pick well. Examine and test to see if they have the gifts and skills you really need and don't just assume they do. Appendix 2 can help you do this.

I want to tell you about Hannah, a lady in one of our church plants. She is seriously active in the church, gets involved in everything she can, is intentional with the ladies in the community and has been driving the parents-and-toddlers work in Bingham, Scotland, for over a year. She is teachable and a real blessing to her church-plant family and the community she serves. Recently, she has started attending the 20schemes Women's training events, and every time I see her it makes me smile. Why tell you about Hannah?

Hannah was originally part of Niddrie, and to my utter shame I have to say she was overlooked. At Niddrie we have a larger congregation, with many seriously capable and gifted women, and it's all too easy to overlook those who are quieter and more in the background. Hannah's care needs were met at Niddrie, but her real potential only came to light in a situation where she had room to grow and be stretched. There is nothing wrong with the same old faces who always want to serve, and we are thankful they turn up. But, we must pause and ask ourselves, are they doing tasks and roles they aren't really gifted for? Are they filling a space a 'Hannah' in our congregation has been waiting to fill? I suspect there are many in our congregations desperate to serve but seeing no opportunities to do so. I'm not remotely suggesting we should get rid of the old faithfuls (they are needed). However, if God has saved us for a purpose and if every member has a role in the body, then we must pay attention and create some space to give other women the opportunity to try.

## The Plan
At last I had what I thought might be a workable plan. I was asked to attend the elders' meeting and present my outline and the list of women for feedback. As we walked through the outline, they asked many questions. These were helpful, enabling me to think

through the reality of the plan and the choice of women. They asked me to explain some of the women and even suggested an additional name. If I'm being honest, I thought this would be the hardest part, but in truth my elders were supportive and the tweaks they asked me to make were helpful additions.

Up to this point, I had not approached the women on my list. That evening, after prayer, the elders gave me permission to do so. This is when the real work began.

## Persuading the Care Team

In my naivety, I thought persuading the women wouldn't be hard. I imagined they had all been sitting in the pews for years frustrated at the lack of opportunity, as I had been. How wrong I was! I approached those I knew would say yes – the easy targets – and after a little chat, thankfully, they were in.

For others, it was a longer process. I spoke to each woman individually, laying out the plan, answering their questions and discussing their fears. Many had fair concerns. Even though there was a plan, it was a fluid one and wasn't written in stone; after all, the idea in my head might not actually work in reality. Committing to something new was hard enough, but I was asking them to commit to a good idea, one we would finalise together. Their fears were legitimate: they felt they didn't know enough or they weren't godly enough. Some lacked confidence, asking, 'Do you really mean me?' I met with each lady (some several times), talked through their fears and concerns, and gave them time to think and pray. Then we talked some more. All but one said yes. These women became my focus for the next two years.

## Training the Care Team

I have an extremely low boredom threshold. I love the challenge of sorting out a mess, being in the mix of a crisis and building something new. But when something is running smoothly, I get bored. As long as I can remember, this has pretty much been my mode of operation, and nowhere shows this side of my character more than my CV. Historically I have taken on two-year contracts with homeless charities. I go in, set something up, learn new skills and move on. It's fairly standard for funders and trusts to give a two- or three-year contract for a post, but it's also common in fundraising to extend contracts. I have always been offered extensions but never took them. Looking back, I can see how this has created a bedrock of required skills and depth of knowledge about foundational structures that has given me the skills required for the role God has for me today. These skills and habits fuelled my thinking when approaching the task of developing a training framework for the women's ministry at NCC and eventually 20schemes.

During the initial conversations with the care team, a question rolled around my head: 'How can I train them and find a way for them to practise their skills without letting them loose on the general congregation before they are ready?'

How would I train them? What would I use to help them build their confidence while encouraging them trust God and to step out of their comfort zone? I spent ages looking for a helpful resource to train the care team. I ended up frustrated when I couldn't find something biblical, practical, interactive and relevant to our context. In the end, I decided I would have to combine a few things: Christian Counseling and Educational

Foundation's (CCEF) How People Change video course, plus a mixture of case studies, topical files and practice.

### Format
We planned to meet as a group monthly for training, mentoring and prayer. This small-group structure worked well for everyone and gave the care team an opportunity to get to know each other on a deeper level.

### CCEF's How People Change Course
CCEF's How People Change course is an excellent resource in many ways, biblically solid and robust, and practical in the way it's set out and great for helping women think through how to speak well into situations. It deals with great truths, such as why we are reluctant to challenge people and whom we are really serving with our fears. On the surface, it looked perfect for us, but in truth it didn't really hit the mark as it comes from a counselling, rather than ongoing pastoral care, culture. It became evident by week three that I would have to start re-writing it for our needs and for our context. The course is embedded within a suburban, middle-class American church culture. In hindsight, I don't know why I thought it would be perfect for us. By the end of the first year, I had rewritten, tweaked and made my own version, which went through several revisions and became a six-module course. Even this wasn't completely satisfactory. Eventually when we launched 20schemes we tossed it and wrote our own training.

### Case studies
How could we teach the women to do one-to-one discipleship without really letting them loose on people until they were ready?

The solution came to me one night: practise on fake people. This is exactly what we did as I created a series of case studies that taught multiple lessons and drip-fed information (because that's what happens in real life: people never tell you the whole story, everything at once; sometimes to start with they don't even tell you the truth at all for that matter). These case studies gave the girls the confidence to make mistakes without causing any harm.

Let's look at this example case study about a girl named 'Brenda':

*Brenda, a Case Study*

*Brenda has been coming to the church since she was a baby. Her parents have been active members in the church, and her father is a deacon. She gave her heart to Christ when she was 10. But although she spent time in Sunday school she found it hard being a kid in church; there simply weren't a lot of kids her age. She was a bit of a loner at school and always felt left out. She struggled through the teenage years, and her relationship with her mum and dad was somewhat strained. She often hit out with bursts of anger at them. When she was 17, she recommitted her life. She has been attending church regularly and is active in her small group (although it was felt she should attend a different group from her parents). She got older and attended college and its Christian Union. People joined the church, and she grew to have a good circle of Christian friends. Last year, when she was 23, she met Jim at a friend's house party. They hit it off straight away. Jim's been a Christian for four years and attends a different church, but he has been to Niddrie visiting a few times and is a regular at Brenda's house for Sunday lunch with her family.*

*Jim is Brenda's first real boyfriend and they have been dating six months.*

*After one really challenging sermon, you see Brenda crying as she heads for the toilet. During coffee you grab the chance to sit with her and ask her how she's doing. She starts to cry again. Realising she isn't going to stop, and is starting to draw some attention, you move her gently into the prayer room for some privacy. After some time, she starts to tell you that she and Jim have been struggling with their relationship. You allow her to talk, and she reveals there have been times when they have struggled and have been intimate with each other. She is overwhelmed, and she starts to cry again. This time she can't stop sobbing, 'I can't believe we went that far...'*

*You are sitting in the prayer room with Brenda.*

1. *What is your immediate response?*
2. *What do you think is going on here?*
3. *What are some of the questions you will ask her?*
4. *How do you bring the Bible to bear in this situation?*
5. *How would you take care of Brenda long term?*

I would use basic questions to start discussion with the care team women and share ideas about how best to speak to Brenda. I purposely left Brenda's story vague. What did the group assume she and her boyfriend were doing? Practically everyone decided, 'They must have slept together!' On the surface it may seem that Brenda and Jim may be having sex, but that's not what she actually says. We don't know enough; we don't know what 'too far' for Brenda actually means. We can't assume, but we need to ask questions and gather the information before we speak.

Case studies enabled me to create situations and scenarios specific to our context and gave the framework to teach the skills the care team women needed. They worked far better than I even imagined, and I have used them in many situations. In a mixed setting with both men and women it's been a really helpful tool to bring to light the different thinking and perspective of each group with surprising results.

## *Topical files*

Making a list of topics women in the church and the schemes had to face on a daily basis, I did some research and found helpful information: journal articles, booklets and so forth. Even after much condensing, this was just too much for people to read. How could we ensure we kept training and sharing knowledge without overburdening the care team? In the end, I created sessions looking at topics from a biblical perspective.

Over time, this format evolved into our monthly fraternal. Our fraternal is available for any woman who is part of a church plant core team, is in ministry with 20schemes or is a ministry wife. The main teaching session, on a variety of topics such as domestic abuse, fear of man or parenting, is delivered by our women's workers as part of their ongoing training. This is then followed by an interactive activity or case study. The format of the training really works well and has, as with all things, evolved over time.

If I'm being honest, I made up this part of the training as we went along, but I like to use the word *fluid* because it sounds far more organised and organic. There was a plan, but I held it loosely. With a fluid structure, I was not constrained or dictated to by the idea and plan. Instead, the structure evolved into what it needed to be. I think this is an important point that has to be made. All too often we find a resource and stick to it rigidly no matter if it fits the need and context.

### *Practice*

At some point, the ladies had to start doing one-to-ones, so we started with each other. Either Miriam McConnell or I had been doing their one-to-ones, but this had to change as our care team members were paired up for one-anothering. This was an equal relationship and not the standard Titus 2 format (older women discipling younger women). In the early days, I would still check in with the girls individually to see how this was going, catch any problems and generally support them as they found their feet. Looking back, this probably was one of the most significant things I did for the care team. We were all considered equals and shared the load, establishing deep and meaningful relationships that have provided support as they have discipled and mentored others.

### *Sharing the load*

I would like to tell you sharing the load was one of my best ideas, but in truth it was originally born out of necessity. I simply didn't have enough time in the day for everything, and I needed help. But don't let the origin detract from the fact that this actually turned out to be one of our greatest strengths. In the early days, after we worked out what we needed from the women's ministry at Niddrie, we came up with a clear list of tasks. These tasks were distributed amongst the members of the care team. Allocation was determined by personal gifting and time availability.

Looking back, it's easy to see the Lord's hand all over this as each care team member had one focus to drive forward. What evolved was something very different than intended, and, frankly, stronger. This is a take-home lesson for three reasons: first, because the tasks were led by people's gifts, it meant we got the best version of what they could be. As the women developed and drove their section of the ministry forward, it grew naturally and was stronger. Second, because each task grew organically and was driven by individual women, it became what was needed and not just what we expected. Lastly, as with so much of the women's ministry I have seen in other places, we weren't dependent on just one person.

The danger of a one-woman band is simply that the ministry revolves around her as it grows. In a sense, it becomes dependent on her driving and developing it. When she leaves, the void that is created takes eons to fill, and for many, when a new worker appears, it can feel like starting over from scratch. This stop-start approach isn't helpful for the congregation. However, our ministry was split between a team where, when someone left and moved on, the ministry continued with others taking on the task and roles. It was natural. In a sense, our congregation didn't feel the loss. Clearly, they felt the loss as someone they cared about moved and they missed them, but it didn't impact the ministry.

Our women's ministry has been serving our congregation for over a decade, and we have had four women coordinators. But each time a change happened the ministry to our congregation was continuous. Our congregation didn't feel the impact other than missing a loved one. This unexpected outcome has enabled us to keep our structure fixed but our delivery flexible.

All in all, the care team's initial focused training took a year. We spent a further year meeting monthly for care and support. It might seem crazy to you that I focused on only a small group of women for such a long time when I was supposed to be growing a ministry. But this is a tried and tested biblical model, one that was exampled by Christ, who also intentionally focused on and taught a small group of disciples, preparing and equipping them for ministry.

We continually review our care team and today we have nine ladies. Several are from the original group, but, as others moved on, thankfully we have had some young new blood to dilute the oldies like me. All new care team members are expected to undertake the Women's Ministry Training Course to ensure we equip them for the role they are about to undertake.

## Appendix Toolkit

* Appendix 2: Evaluating Members' Gifting Toolkit

## Further Resources

* Melissa Kruger, *Growing Together: Taking Mentoring beyond Small talk and Prayer Requests* (Crossway, 2020)
* Timothy Lane & Paul Tripp, *How People Change*, 3rd ed. (New Growth Press, 2007)

# 5

---

# There Will Be Trouble Ahead

I would love to tell you I implemented Niddrie's women's ministry without any real mistakes, but I would be lying. It was not all smooth sailing. I think I made so many mistakes I could fill a whole book of stories and anecdotes that would leave me horrified and red faced. The reality is, I am sinful, made errors and learnt many painful lessons as I organised the ministry. In this chapter, I want to focus on just a few of those lessons.

My hope in writing this chapter is twofold. First, so you may avoid making the same mistakes. Second, so you won't be afraid to make a mistake. Mistakes usually bring our greatest lessons. We need to learn to fail well. What I mean is it's inevitable you will stuff up at some point. When that happens, admit your fault, repent and get back in the game.

## Being Impatient
Do you remember playing sports at school and the teacher would

line you up against the wall as teams were picked? The two team leaders would stand there calling out a name, and every kid was praying they weren't last. All the obvious kids got picked first – some because they were good at the game, and others because the team captain was their pal. Ultimately, there was always one wee kid left who no one wanted. I remember those days well, and I didn't want the selection of the care team to feel like this.

God has saved all Christians for a purpose and given each of us gifts to serve the body, but that doesn't mean we all have the same gifts. We know this to be true from verses such as 1 Corinthians 12:12, 'Just as a body, though one, has many parts, but all its many parts form one body, so it is with Christ.' Unfortunately, all too often we hold particular roles and gifting in higher esteem than others, and we end up coveting and desiring that role and ministry. Many times, I have heard people tell me they think they are gifted women's workers, and in time it becomes apparent they sadly miss the mark. This is why it's so important we provide opportunities for women to use, practise and discover their gifting.

One of the biggest mistakes I made when picking the team was undervaluing how it would feel to be left on the shelf. One lady had a horrendous time dealing with this, and it impacted her one-to-one relationship for a number of years. I didn't deal with it as well as I should have. I flitted between placating her and navigating around the issue. I tried to give her tasks in an attempt to make her feel more useful. We had many meetings where we would discuss the situation. I would be honest and frank, but not always gentle. There were times when I was plainly frustrated and wanted her to grow up and get over herself. I struggle with women I see as high-maintenance or needy; over time I have had to really work on my sinfully dismissive, unloving attitude.

In this case, though, I mostly lacked patience. She genuinely was a lovely woman who was seriously gifted in many other areas. I should have been far more patient and gracious with her. In time, she did learn how to be more intentional, pastorally aware and developed in this area. In hindsight, though, I sometimes wonder how different the road would have been for both of us if I had brought her with me instead of dragging her into line.

## Fear of Man

Working for my church has definitely melted my head in a number of ways, but nothing overcame me so much as fear of man. Allowing other people's opinions to rule me doesn't quite hit the right note, as it was more than that: I allowed what I *thought* people's opinions were of me to rule me. I know, twisted! There were lots of things that fed into my thinking, such as my congregation was paying my salary, the perceived and imagined expectations, people wanting to be friends because they think you have some sort of inside scope on everything going on in church, or, worst of all, knowing things you can't unhear. I assumed I had to be at every meeting, I was concerned about taking time off and what hours I worked that week, and I was reluctant to claim expenses. I became paranoid about what I said, being careful about my words and then analysing them afterward to work out any damage I might have done. This exhausted me.

Some of my concerns weren't imagined, sadly. There have been times when people have said hurtful things to my face.

Someone once told me that since I was working for the church I was held to a higher standard and they expected better from me than the rest. Sometimes it felt like living in a goldfish bowl.

Whether these fears were real or perceived, being ruled by anything or anyone other than God was unhelpful. I remember the day it finally dawned on me. I was in the café, upset at my pastor Mez for some reason I can't even remember – something to do with ministry. The only bit I actually remember of the conversation is him saying, 'Wait! You're reacting to what you *think* I'm going to say. I don't even know what we're talking about!' Even though I hate to admit it, he was absolutely right, and when I reflected on it, I realised I did this a lot. This was the beginning of a recurring conversation in the early days of accountability with Miriam. I have repented of and talked and prayed about this sin. It's a carbuncle that, when I think it has been lanced and mended, comes back out of the blue. I have been seeing Miriam for one-anothering for over a decade now; she knows me very well. I'm grateful she cares enough to call me out on this sin and other recurring sinful habits that are more deeply imbedded and have taken time to eradicate.

One of the other things fuelled by fear of man was my horrendous habit of comparing myself to others. It wasn't others in general but specifically the women I judged to be super-Christians who could do my job better than me. I had been in ministry for over a decade when, while writing a session called Passing on the DNA for our women's ministry course, I suddenly realised it didn't matter who was my best choice – I was God's choice. The DNA of our ministry would look very different with someone else driving it.

## Pride

I remember a long time ago when our now pastor Andy Constable was a young assistant and was just stepping out to lead the team, handling the day-to-day on his own for an extended hunk of time. We were in a team meeting, and he communicated something to me in front of the team that I didn't find palatable. It wasn't really what he said, more how he said it and that he hadn't really listened to me. Inside I was quietly raging. I left the meeting and got in my car, but before I had driven two minutes, I started the internal conversation. I knew my reaction was sinful, but what sin was in the driving seat? I quickly asked my favourite get-to-the-heart-of-the-matter question. What is it I want that I'm not getting in this situation? Respect! I felt Andy had not been respectful and given me my due. Pride was really at the root of my emotions.

Quickly, I started repenting, praying and rebuking my attitude. How well was I loving Andy at this moment? It was his first time stepping up, it was a massive responsibility to run the team and the day-to-day ministry, and here I was dwelling on my own self-importance instead of being useful to him. I spent the rest of the journey asking the Lord to help me love and serve him well. I wanted to be a help, not a hindrance.

Later that day, I found out he was needing to have a difficult conversation with someone. He was struggling with what he had to do, and that's why he was distracted in the meeting. No one likes being the bad guy. Thankfully, my sinful response had been internalised and hadn't added to his burden. Pride is a killer to any team.

## Discontentment

I was in the car with Miriam McConnell on our way to a shop. As we drove there, I ranted the whole way. Then I ranted the whole time we were in the shop and even on the journey back. Miriam listened and annoyingly said I had to speak to Mez. This was the last thing I wanted to do, thank you very much.

I feel this attitude was my standard in ministry for at least the first five years (Miriam may suggest it was more). I became less 'ranty' over time, and I would get to the heart of the issue in three minutes instead of three hours. But the heart issue was the same. I had become vanilla (or, as Miriam would call it, more mature) instead of rocky road in my demeanour. At the heart of my moaning and whinging was always discontentment. I was not happy about what God had asked me to do and definitely was not trusting him. I actually can't believe how much time I wasted wishing myself somewhere else.

It took me a long time to realise the root of my discontentment (and my fear of man and my self-reliance) was a lack of trust in the Lord. I trusted the Lord with some things, but not everything.

## Speaking Without Thought or Wisdom

Speaking without thought or wisdom is probably the thing I regret the most. There are a plethora of examples of when I was quick to speak and slow to listen. I'm always quick to apologise, even when people don't know what I'm talking about (I know my heart state). But there is one moment, one person, I will always think about with regret. She would be my do-over if such things existed.

This particular person came to our church with her kids. She was coming from a church that had a nice, evangelical and solid minister, but a mixed bag of a congregation. I spent time with her, and found out she was leaving her existing church because she had an issue, a conflict, with one of the ladies there. She asked me what I thought. I don't remember exactly what I said, but I know the basic thread. She should leave her previous church well. She needed to sort it out with this lady first before she considered leaving there. In time, she did stop coming to Niddrie and returned to her original church. Years later, she is nowhere with the Lord. She was immature in faith, and I should have cared for her and her children better. I should have left her alone in Niddrie and fed into her. Now, I know God is sovereign and in control. I know any that are truly his return; I know he chooses whom he saves, not me. I was so concerned about doing what was right theoretically that I forgot to do what was right for this situation.

## Self-Reflection

I know not each of your sinful hearts will be fuelled by the same sins I have mentioned. You may not have an issue with fear of man, pride, discontentment or word-vomit arrows. You will have your own battle to contend with. Being involved in ministry doesn't give you superpowers that protect you from sin or from making mistakes. How you handle your mistakes and deal with your sinfulness will say much about your character.

Spend some time reflecting on the following questions:

1. What do you think your mistakes will say about your character?
2. What recurring imbedded sin do you constantly have to repent of? How is this impacting you personally and your ministry?
3. How can you ensure you stay teachable?
4. How can you and your care team care for each other well?
5. Are you prepared to be honest, vulnerable and open with your care team? How do you plan to promote and cultivate this culture within the group?

Many of us have a tendency to dwell, even brood, when things go wrong, especially when we are the ones who have stuffed up. We may even analyse and go over everything in our heads, trying to work out how we could have dealt with the situation better. Refection can be helpful if it's done well. I remember an intern who was behaving in an unacceptable way, basically thinking they were invincible. I was angry and frustrated, and I ran out of patience. They had taken liberties for the last time, so I dealt with it – badly! Mez saw all this and allowed me to go wading in like a bulldozer and then said, 'So, how do you think you could have handled that better?' I already knew I had handled it badly. There were about a million ways I could have handled that better. Mez allowed me to make my mistake because it was a lesson I needed to learn the hard way.

I didn't have to reflect for long to know what needed to be changed. Obviously, I apologised publicly to the intern, who was surprised I would do such a thing. Remember, as mature women of God we are to be an example of how to deal with the sinful mistakes we make. Dwelling on this, beating myself up and throwing a pity party would have been pointless, self-indulgent and immature. It's actually one of the indicators I use when assessing our potential women workers. I'm more interested in how she handles her mistakes than the mistakes themselves. If she tries to hide her behaviour, isn't completely forthright when challenged or makes excuses and takes no responsibility, this hints she might not be the person for the job. We must model and look for biblical character and teachability: 'Whoever conceals their sins does not prosper, but the one who confesses and renounces them finds mercy' (Prov. 28:13).

You will make mistakes, and you will respond sinfully. But what is your character made of?

# 6

# On the Receiving End

In ministry it's not only my personal mistakes that have proved to be teachers; there were times when I was on the receiving end and learning from others' mistakes. I don't mind sharing where I have been at fault, but I am loath to share stories involving others. I have wrestled with this, and largely avoided it. The truth is, no matter how much I change someone's name to hide their identity, people may work it out, and that makes me uncomfortable. So, for those reading this who think they are Niddrie's answer to Miss Marple, please keep your guesses to yourself.

## Getting Burnt

There have been many times when I have been burnt in ministry. What I mean is I have experienced painful times because of someone else's actions, such as theft, lies, rumours, etc. From this kind of burn I have found the healing process isn't the hardest thing to deal with; it's the temptation to get cynical and carry your baggage to the next person. This affects how many risks you are prepared to take and how you respond to people you are called to serve.

A long time ago, we had a very serious situation – it nearly broke me. I genuinely never thought it would come to an end. I can't share the details because at the time my elders asked me not to speak about it for the other party's protection. I was not to engage in any conversation about the situation or discuss it with anyone. To this day, I have not, not even to Miriam as my one-to-one. One of my best friends refused to speak to me after this incident, because she felt I was being secretive, guarded and dishonest and it showed I didn't trust her. Our friendship hasn't been rekindled even though we have been reconciled as believers and have spoken since.

I am not going to describe what actually happened, but suffice to say, there had been undercurrents of trouble and issues going on for ages. It was a nightmare of a situation that finally erupted in an official complaint against me. I didn't know what the complaint was. No one spoke to me or told me what was going on, no one asked me for an account of my side. I was simply told there was a serious issue, and I couldn't speak about it. Meanwhile everyone else knew some version, because the complainant went around telling everyone and anyone who would listen (including people I knew from other churches). With each telling, the story became more elaborate. Still I couldn't speak. No matter what the complainant said, and to whom (even my closest friends), I wasn't allowed to say anything. I was getting burnt alive and silently smiling whilst being roasted. This went on for months. It was horrendous.

One night one of the elders called me at home for a discussion. I eventually got up the nerve and asked him if I was allowed to know what I was being accused of. He told me. Turns out a letter I was asked to write, which had been checked by an elder before sending, didn't go down well with the complainant. In all truth it wasn't about the letter; it was just the focus for the attack.

In time I was fully exonerated, but the complainant went on to greater, more divisive and destructive things before finally moving on.

The hardest thing I had to do was stay silent and never defend myself; I had to trust God. It was difficult not to explain myself even to my closest friends, and I feared they would believe the lies about me. I had to trust they knew me well enough to know how I would really act.

This wasn't the first complaint lodged with my elders about me. Early on, I was meeting a lady for a one-to-one. One day I challenged her sinful behaviour. We talked and prayed. When I left, I made sure she was really fine, and she assured me she was and thanked me. We hugged and off I went. She called her husband hysterically crying, and he called my elders to complain about me.

On my way to work the next day, my phone rang. I remember pulling over to return the call. It was about the woman whose husband had complained about me. I listened, sighed, listened some more. I sat in my car for a good 10 minutes before I could bring myself to move. I remember my thoughts: 'What is the point? I could be at home with my kids instead of navigating this mess!' I nearly turned around and chucked it in. You see, I was tired and worn out from the night before which had been knee-deep in drama. Along with Mez, I had spent the evening with a woman from the scheme who was frantic. Her partner, a professing new believer, was drunk; it was all very ugly. And now comes a complaint against me. Why even bother?

The next Sunday after this incident, the lady who had complained via her husband caught me in the corridor at church, she apologised for her behaviour and said she didn't know why she had lied. Thankfully I had forgiven her quickly after the event, so this conversation was easy to have. God used this situation to change both me and this couple. Fast-forward a decade later, and the husband asked to speak to me. I'll admit my heart sank. I thought, 'What have I done now?' (I told you I have a recurring battle with fear of man.) His opening sentence surprised me: 'I don't know if you remember this, but…' He then went on to share about the incident that happened a decade ago. He finished with something along the lines of, 'I hope you realise we aren't the same people we were back then,' and apologised for what happened. They aren't the same people, and neither am I. I was actually stunned. The event was years ago, and there was no animosity between us. But he was convicted and responding to that. I share this story to remind the girls why we should persevere: we don't know what God's doing. We just have to keep trusting him. It's basically the number one lesson.

## Isolation

I remember my second week on staff at Niddrie Community Church. Mez said to me, 'Are your rose-tinted glasses off yet?' It's true I had an idealised image of my congregation. There are things I know now that I can't unhear, and I hate it. I have heard and seen things that can't be scooped out of my brain.

I don't know why I was surprised; it's not like I was the only one in the membership who sinned. I was self-sin-aware, but I liked to believe an ideal about everyone else. There are some people who like to know all the gossip, but I hate it. The thing about being on staff is that people either think you know what they have been up to, or they *know* you know (even when I don't). I don't know if this felt worse because I had been a member of the church for years prior to my role. But, when you are involved in many of the crisis moments, the difficult discipline moments or are party to disclosures that need to be addressed, suddenly it feels like you are Jessica Fletcher on *Murder She Wrote*. Let's face it, everyone she knows gets charged with murder – if you knew her, you would avoid her. It can feel the same being the women's worker, and, I suspect, probably the pastor's wife. Then there are the people who want to befriend you because they think you have the inside scoop. It can be isolating.

I actually understand this from the opposite side as well. Earlier, I mentioned Mez decided we were all going to practise accountability with each other. I may have said yes on the outside, but inside I didn't want to reveal my life and struggles to the pastor's wife. If I had the choice, I would have avoided accountability by being superficial and nice while surface skimming topics and evading depth during our conversations. Polite Christianity can be very isolating.

If I'm truly being honest, though, isolating myself is very tempting. I used to be an extrovert, but now I have swung the opposite direction. The lie I tell myself is that isolation is safe. If you aren't there, you can't hear it, no one will expect anything from you and you don't have to constantly think before speaking. All of which is exhausting. One of my real pleasures is being able to speak to someone *safe* (thankfully there are a few) with complete abandonment. True, unadulterated and honest Shabba without having to guard, think or be mindful of the weight my words may carry.

That's why I'm so thankful for the women's ministry team, especially those who have been there from the beginning – being there for me with tough love when I need it, but also ice cream and chocolate when that's needed. The whole team are family, and I am totally loved by them. They have my back, they care and they are always there. There is not a chance to be isolated with that crew.

Lastly, having trustworthy, faithful friends outside of Niddrie is important. I can't even remember who gave me this gem of advice, but it's so valuable. Hanging out with some friends who aren't in ministry or in my church is such a breath of fresh air, as well as fun. I try to hang out with each of my non-Niddrie friends at least once a month (sometimes more, sometimes less), but my point is I make the effort.

## Frustration

There are many frustrations in women's work. In this last section, I want to reflect on an ongoing frustration that I am still trying to learn from – why can't I convince the older women to disciple younger women?

I genuinely don't know if we have made mistakes in our process of recruiting older women to mentor young women, but I do know we have tried almost everything we can possibly think of without any real success. This isn't just a 'me' thing either. I remember reading a chapter on this subject in *Word-Filled Women's Ministry* edited by Gloria Furman and Kathleen Nielson. It was a discussion in the form of a letter from an older woman, Susan Hunt, responding to a younger woman's difficulties of getting someone older to mentor her. Our care team had been talking about and trying to deal with this same problem without any change. For a long time, I was the oldest lady in our congregation who would do a one-to-one with someone. After reading the chapter, I immediately emailed two others in the church and sent them the book. 'Let's knock our heads together and make a plan,' I said.

I would love to tell you we have been able to enlist older women to disciple younger women. But, and I don't know why, we have made no significant inroads into this in over a decade of trying. The most exciting thing that happened was last year one of the ladies in our congregation, Catherine, retired and has wonderfully stepped up. She meets with several women now. I hope she will encourage other older women of the faith to take a step toward discipling.

We have some very gifted and mature older ladies who will serve in practical ways (making tea, washing dishes, or crèche). But if you ask them to join our care team, they would say no.

One older lady at church is very sociable, friendly and really good at getting to know newbies and young Christians. In the last decade she has grown in her faith, knowledge and maturity and could now helpfully speak into others' lives. She has had a one-to-one relationship since coming to Niddrie, so for many years she has been receiving from someone else but won't give to others. For about five years we have been having the same conversation about her stepping up. Even last Monday the same thing happened. She said to me, 'I've been reading Mez's book about service, and I'm challenged again! So I'm praying about where God wants me to serve.' Same conversation, but no matter what support, care and encouragement we give to her, nothing changes. Why? I have been asking this question for years. Is it fear, lack of training or lack of confidence? Though the care team have asked questions, had discussions and made several plans, nothing changes.

It has taken me a long time to realise maybe it's a generational thing. What I mean is these women are from the generation that thinks of service as practical acts. These women are serving well, and I need to remember that. Making tea, running crèche, washing dishes, and cleaning the church are significant and important forms of service, and I don't want to diminish that. Love is needed, especially in these areas of frustration.

I also had to acknowledge that at the heart of my frustration may have been my sinful impatience. There is a season for everything and at the right time God will bring about change, if it's needed, not me or the ten different initiatives I put in place to make it happen.

## Appendix Toolkit

• Appendix 3: Guarding Your Heart

# PART 2

---

*'Do not merely listen to the word, and so deceive yourselves.*
*Do what it says' (Jas. 1:22).*

# 7

## Loving Others Enough to Share the Gospel

A couple of years ago, I decided to join the local gym. I wanted to get fit and meet new women from my community. I had been thinking for a while about how I could engage with women in Niddrie who work and thus whom I never got a chance to meet during the day. The local gym was my solution. I met a few women in one of the classes, and we got chatting about the usual stuff: work, kids, boyfriends or lack thereof. I tried to be intentional by taking the same classes at the same time, usually with the same people, and, as I got to know them better, praying for them by name. The Lord was good. I had several chats, some opportunities to share my testimony and one evil spin class that led to serious questions about being a Christian.

There I was at the spin class, barely able to talk, sweat dripping on the floor and the ladies flinging question after question at me. The concept of discussing why Christians don't 'try before they buy' when it comes to husbands, whilst trying to follow the instructor, made my legs scream and my head melt. Spin and interrogation about how I live my life as a Christian had not been on my to-do list for that night. It wasn't a pretty sight, but it was a great class! Nothing was forced; most of the time it felt like the ladies had been wanting to ask me questions for ages. It would have been so much easier to just fly under the radar and be another face in the crowd. Sure, I was there to get fit so I put the work in, but I didn't see it as my primary goal or my special 'me time'. I didn't leave Jesus behind when I signed in. A deliberate life, intentionally lived, can bring amazing opportunities to share the gospel.

## The Right Question to Ask

Being a women's worker is more than working with and serving Christians. It involves evangelism too. And yet this isn't something that always comes easily. A question I get asked a lot is, 'How do you engage with women?' But unless you are one of those rare women who works from home, does all her shopping and banking online and only talks via text, Zoom or email, then in some way you are engaging with people. True, some of us do this on a deeper level than others. I acknowledge some people are more inept than others at social interaction, but, realistically, unless you're Tom Hanks in the movie *Castaway* and stranded with Wilson the volleyball as your sole friend, then you are, in life, engaging with women.

I think we are asking the wrong question. I think the question we should be asking is, 'Why don't I share the gospel with women?' How deliberate are you at sharing the gospel whilst you engage in the world around you? And if you're not being intentional, then why not? We can take courses on evangelism –

even run courses on evangelism, work out fancy questionnaires or read amazing books about the gospel, but at some point we are going to have to open our mouths and share about the hope we have.

Pause for just a minute and reflect. Ask yourself, 'Why don't I share the gospel?'

One reoccurring phrase I hear is, 'It wasn't the right time to share; they aren't there yet.' Is that really what's going on, or is it more likely you don't share because you're scared? Maybe you are fearful they may ask you a hard question or they will reject you. Another reoccurring phrase I hear in people's own defence is, 'I invite loads of people to church.' Good for you, but inviting someone to church isn't sharing the gospel. One of the most heartbreaking things I often hear is, 'I just like to show people Jesus loves them.' Usually this statement is from people who are serving in some form of ministry such as a soup kitchen or debt advice service, but women's workers can fall into the same trap. My heart breaks because, without the whole gospel, this act of love feeds their bellies or sorts their finances (today's physical needs) but doesn't meet their greatest and deepest need of being reconciled to God (spiritual need). It's temporary and not eternal.

Stuart Olyott said in his commentary on Romans, 'much of what passes for the "gospel" today is not the gospel of God at all'.[1] Not pulling his punches, Olyott goes on a few pages later to say the 'main reason for the weakness of today's church is that the gospel which is believed in the pew, and which is proclaimed by ordinary men and women, bears little resemblance to the

---

1. Stuart Olyott, *Romans: The Gospel as It Really Is* (Evangelical Press, 1997), p. 11.

gospel contained in the epistle to the Romans'.[2] Sadly, what passes for many as evangelism is social assistance and not the truth of how people stand before God and their eternal jeopardy. When we meet the physical need without consideration for the spiritual need, something needs to be addressed.

When thinking about evangelism – or encouraging others in it – we need to do two things. First, we have to know the gospel clearly and share it concisely. Inviting someone to church, saying you will pray for someone and sharing a thoughtful verse is nice, but it is not the gospel and it is not evangelism. Second, we have to get over ourselves. We need to love and care about the eternal consequences of our friends and families more than we care about ourselves. We need to love them enough to tell them the offensive truth of the gospel no matter how they feel about us afterwards (1 Cor. 1:18).

## The "How" Is Important Too

We do, however, need to think about how we go about sharing Jesus. I remember years back I was walking through the local shopping mall and this woman walked up to me with a pile of tracts and said, 'Have you been washed in the blood of the Lamb?' I don't even know where to start when it comes to this evangelistic approach other than to say don't use it. She may have loved the Lord, but, other than a Christian, who understands that question? It was a strange interaction, and, even as someone who had been washed in the blood of the Lamb, I was looking for the nearest exit. We need to share the gospel without being strange and off-putting in the process. That's sometimes harder than we think.

2. Ibid. p. 15.

Personally, I'm just not one of those people who can sit down with someone and within minutes share the gospel. However, just because I don't have that gift doesn't mean I get a special waiver from sharing the gospel. When we are hanging out with people we know (family, colleagues, friends, gym buddies, mums at the school gates), eventually we talk about what we really care about: our kids, our hobbies, our pets or maybe even church. But many of us find it hard to get past vague details about church to the specifics of the gospel. Why is that? If Jesus is so important to us, why can't we talk about him? If Jesus is such an important part of our lives, then it should be just as natural, easy and normal talking about him as it is talking about your kids, cat, new boyfriend or latest diet kick.

## Connecting Well

Problems can occur when we are trying to engage women in an unnatural setting with no natural connection or pre-existing relationship. Maybe as a mum you have organised a play date for your kids with the quirky kid at school who everyone avoids but you make your kids be nice to. The play date never goes well as they sit and stare at each other whilst you silently will your kids to be nice. Everyone is grateful when it's over. The temptation when there isn't a natural connection, or a pre-existing relationship, is to force one or find a way to make one happen. But it doesn't have to be strange or convoluted. As I have said, no one is Tom Hanks in *Castaway*. Sometimes we just need to work out how we fit into the jigsaw that is our context. We can figure that out by asking ourselves some questions.

1. Do you know where the women in your community spend their time?
2. What common connectors are there?

   Maybe your kids go to the same school; you like art and there is a class at your local community centre; a local charity shop needs volunteers; you like to swim and there is a local swimming group on Facebook; you live next door to each other.
3. Do you know what they are afraid of or, alternatively, what makes them laugh?
4. Do you know the name of your regular coffee barista, the school crossing guard or your hairdresser? Who can you be praying for by name?
5. Do you know the patterns of your community?

We can't underestimate the opportunity ordinary moments in life offer, such as a lift to an appointment, a hand with the shopping or even help to cut the grass. I met Natasha because she was the daughter of a friend of mine, and every time I spotted her at a bus stop I would pull over and offer her a lift to where she was going. One time I offered her a lift and she said, 'I'm not getting in your car if you're going to give me the God chat!' Laughing, I said, 'That's pretty likely. I can't help myself.' Natasha got in the car (she always did) and the 20-minute detour offered me more than one natural opportunity to share the gospel. When we are truly imbedded and invested within our community, and praying for opportunities to share the gospel, don't be surprised when you get the chance. Who knows what God will do. You may get the opportunity to read the Bible with people or see them come to Christ.

You don't have to be gifted; being faithful will do. We may fumble, we might not get the words right and we may even get asked a question we don't know the answer to. Real relationship leads to real gospel opportunities. It's in these moments we pray we get over ourselves and boldly share when the occasions naturally arise. If you wimp out – remember, everyone has missed an opportunity – simply own it and pray for a next time and that you will step up. We have all had moments where we have let our sinful fear of man, pride, arrogance and selfishness get in the way of the perfect opportunity. We have all struggled for words and said the wrong thing. We have all dropped a clanger or even offended someone. There will be these moments. We are imperfect beings sharing the glorious truth. And we should be *sharing*; we should be proclaiming and telling the truth.

At the heart of this chapter is the encouragement to become involved within the community you work and worship in rather than just sticking to discipling the Christians. To connect and find opportunities to share the hope of Christ with people. This bites because it means we must give up our time and share our lives. When we truly start to engage with the women in our community, we start to realise how messy their lives are and how messy *our* lives are.

## Sharing Messy Lives

Everyone struggles to be real, but this can be a really big problem for those of us in some sort of paid ministry – we feel we should be showing people we've got it all together. I remember when my kids were little I had been hanging out with a local lady called Karen. I met her at the school gate, and she started coming to our church. One morning we planned to walk the kids to school together. But the moment she knocked on the door that morning happened to be the very moment I was shouting at my kids about where their school shoes were. So, as I was yelling, 'Why do we have to have this palaver every day?', I dispelled the myth that I had it all together. I sighed inwardly, kicking myself for being such a horrendous example to this woman; yet, on the walk to school, as I was about to apologise, she said to me, 'I thought you always had it all together.' She had this idea that Christians were perfect, never struggled with anything and never raised their voices at their kids. We had a great conversation about my sinfulness and the price Jesus paid for it. I'm not advocating yelling at your kids, but I am encouraging you to bring people into your life, truly inviting them into the reality of your life. That kind of relationship is messy, time-consuming and costly. People see what it really means to be a Christian.

## It's Not Us Who Saves

Before I finish this chapter, I want to just flag something I think we forget. God is the one who saves. It's his job, not ours; all we do is faithfully proclaim. It's so easy to get frustrated when we are consistently sharing the gospel with others, and they just don't get it. We had an older lady who used to come to church. She started coming to our café, then club, then church services. Eventually I was doing a Bible study with her, blatantly sharing the gospel week in and week out for years. Two years to be exact. I remember getting so frustrated, thinking, *What do I need to do to get her to understand the truth?* One day, during what I would say was *the* most boring sermon on the planet (we had a guest speaker), God opened her eyes and she repented that moment. God rebuked me that day, reminding me who was in charge, who has the power to save and who opens ears to hear. It wasn't by any effort of mine but by His divine mercy.

Don't get lost in the evangelism flim-flam; we don't need a fancy training programme or evangelistic event. We simply need to trust the Word of God and the truth of the gospel. We complicate what is simple. Proclaim the whole gospel through word as well as deed. We need to practise what we preach, being doers and not just speakers of the Word (Jas. 1:22–25). We also need to pray. Pray the seed bears fruit and God will mercifully save.

# 8

---

# Titus 2 Discipleship

**Titus 2 Discipleship**

As we start to think about discipleship we are going to focus on Titus 2:3–5. I know there are reams of books, blogs and sermons on this passage. It seems to be one of the go-to places for discipleship. This passage's popularity does not negate that it is a seriously helpful scripture and eloquently describes what discipleship should look like:

> *Older women likewise are to be reverent in behaviour, not slanderers or slaves to much wine. They are to teach what is good, and so train the young women to love their husbands and children, to be self-controlled, pure, working at home, kind, and submissive to their own husbands, that the word of God may not be reviled. (Titus 2:3–5, ESV)*

In this passage we can see two things clearly. First, we see how, as godly and mature women, we are called to behave and live (v. 3). Second, Titus states that we are to teach younger women to do likewise; we are to teach them how to be godly women. Therefore, for this chapter we will follow the format set out in Titus 2 and look at what it means to be a godly example and to teach and disciple younger women. We will then look at some practical ways to go about this Titus 2 relationship.

## Be a Godly Example

At a conference a few years ago, Ed Stetzer said, 'You can't lead what you won't live.' Even though he was talking primarily to a group of pastors, I think this challenge is relevant for us today. What I mean is, as we think through women's discipleship, we must apply the Bible to our own lives as well as speak biblical truth into the lives of those we are discipling. We need to live the Word out, not just speak it. We see this in Romans 2:21–23: 'you, then, who teach others, do you not teach yourself? You who preach against stealing, do you steal? You who say that people should not commit adultery, do you commit adultery? You who abhor idols, do you rob temples? You who boast in the law, do you dishonour God by breaking the law?'

Or as James puts it, 'Do not merely listen to the word, and so deceive yourselves. Do what it says' (Jas. 1:22).

But when it comes to the Christian life, these instructions aren't always reflected. There are times when we are great at pulling out the right verse or chewing over a piece of Scripture, but we aren't actually keen about applying it to our own lives. For many, what comes out of our mouths isn't replicated in our lives. We can even get caught up in what we think a godly woman looks like, with the unfounded expectations many of us have as Christians, and try hard to achieve it. We often have self-imposed expectations that we have to be the perfect Proverbs 31 lady, the Christian superwoman.

In her book *Good News for Weary Women*, Elyse Fitzpatrick asks a few poignant questions of women on Facebook and from focus groups. She asks this: 'What are the dumbest things people tell women they have to do in order to be godly?'[1] Here are some of the answers she got:

- Never disagree with other people – especially not your husband
- Always, always obey the law
- Only read Christian books (or books with a strong Christian moral)
- Always submit – followed by a terrible definition of the word
- Never drink beer, wine or any kind of alcohol (even in moderation)
- Don't allow your children to be exposed to Disney characters
- Godliness means you have to vote a certain way
- Godliness means you have to boycott places that support gay rights
- Stay with an abusive husband even if you feel threatened
- When your children misbehave, you should be able to quote verses to them (or have them recite verses to you)

Fitzpatrick goes on to say,

*Whether we are aware of it or not, we all define ourselves by the rules or laws we keep...many are imposed on us...no matter where these standards originate, once a rule has taken root in our lives,*

1. Elyse Fitzpatrick, *Good News for Weary Women* (Tyndale House, 2014), p. 74.

*it is nearly impossible to extract it, especially if it came with some sort of promised reward or threat of punishment. If we believe that God is pleased by our rule keeping, we will find it difficult to abandon those rules without feeling guilty and fearing that something bad will happen to us if we don't comply.*[2]

All too often we can be sucked into this lie, following the *imposed or imagined* rules and portraying the perfect godly image that everything is alright and that we never struggle with anything, as if we are floating on some wonderful Christian bliss cloud. When we do this, we project a false image of what a good, godly woman looks like and a fake impression of the Christian walk. It's not good or helpful. This isn't a godly life. A godly life isn't one without trial or struggle, but one that examples Christ and our dependence on him in the midst of the trial, standing firm in him: 'Consider it pure joy, my brothers and sisters, whenever you face trials of many kinds, because you know that the testing of your faith produces perseverance. Let perseverance finish its work so that you may be mature and complete, not lacking anything' (Jas. 1:2–4).

Daniel Doriani, in his commentary on James, says, 'Our response to the trial reveals our heart condition.'[3]

### Reflective question

When faced with a trial, what does our response reveal about us? Who are we relying on? Who are we exampling?

---

2. Ibid. p. 74.

3. Daniel Doriani, *James: Reformed Expository Commentary* (P&R Publishing, 2007), p. 15.

As godly, mature women we need to show other women how to deal well with the trials we face. To do that we need to invite them into our lives and homes. Even when our homes are messy and our kids are running riot. They need to see what it looks like for a godly, mature woman to cope well when life is chucking bricks, the kids are kicking off and you're having a bad hair day. One who examples steadfastness, spiritual joy and trust ultimately examples Christ in those moments.

This is where it gets uncomfortable, because all too often we find the façade over our private spaces comfortable. It protects us and our image. We like the idea of discipleship when it's clean, structured and doesn't require too much personal sacrifice. We don't like it when it's messy, demanding and encroaches into our lives.

## Teach and Disciple Women

Titus 2 doesn't leave us in much doubt that, as mature women, we should be investing in younger Christian women. As they grow up in the faith, we need to help them along the way. Be someone of whom they can ask the hard questions, someone who will help unravel unbiblical thinking and someone who will continually point to Christ not only by words but example. Discipleship isn't new; we have as mothers and sisters been teaching the young how to grow up and navigate life forever.

When I taught my son to do the laundry, I didn't just hand him the manual for the machine, a box of laundry detergent and the basket of dirty clothes and say, 'On you go, son.' No, I showed him how to separate the whites from darks, which button to push, how much laundry detergent to use; I walked him through the task. I walked both my kids through all the big life lessons such as cooking, cleaning, relationships, and personal safety. I didn't just leave them to get on with it. I helped them to grow up into mature adults. It's what we do as parents. So why do we see it differently for new or young Christians? We need to help them grow up into mature adult Christians.

Unfortunately, when it comes to helping new believers 'grow up' we hand them a manual (the Bible), give them the odd instruction (during a prayer meeting or Bible study) and let them get on with it. In Christian circles we are so used to the set format of once-a-week Bible studies and prayer meetings as a form of discipleship, but it's simply not enough.

Discipling Christians from an unchurched and potentially chaotic background is difficult. It is not a meet-once-a-week task. It's a 24/7, living-with, walking-alongside and sharing-your-life experience. I will be bold enough to say I don't think a once-a-week approach is enough for any new Christian, no matter the background. Discipleship provides the framework where believers walk through life together with Christ: it is one-to-one relationship; a place to face the tough stuff and deal with our lives' trials within the context of a loving Christian community relationship; encouraging each other to rely on Christ; and speaking his wisdom into everyday situations. Look at the guidance found in James 5:16: 'Therefore confess your sins to each other and pray for each other so that you may be healed. The prayer of a righteous person is powerful and effective.'

In a discipleship relationship we can pray, support, example maturity, strengthen one another, bring comfort, admonish and ultimately point the believer to Christ.

This type of discipleship is costly, and the sad truth is many mature Christians don't want to pay the price. It's so frustrating how few people want to be involved in discipleship. I hear a lot of excuses: I can't do it, I don't have the gifts, I don't know enough about the Lord or I can't help them with any hard problems they might have, and, probably the saddest excuse ever, I just don't have the time in my schedule.

If we are so busy doing our own thing that we can't make space in our schedules to disciple one person, then I humbly suggest there is something seriously wrong with our schedules. The question that floats around my head in these moments is, *Who are we really serving with our time?*

### *Who are you serving with your time?*

I know we are all busy, but maybe we need to be just a bit more inventive about how we go about using our time. I heard this example from Mez McConnell: Most of us eat three meals a day. That's 21 meals a week, approximately 91 meals a month and 1,092 meals a year. If we simply tithe those meals and share them with a younger woman we want to invest in, we aren't adding anything extra to our schedules. I spend breakfast once a week with two women. We work through a devotional, discuss the week's issues, pray and encourage each other in the faith. I'm going to eat, pray and do my quiet time anyway. I'm not changing my schedule just inviting someone else into it and investing. I have benefited from this time as much as they have. Little tweaks can make a big difference, like bringing someone along with you to the gym, shop or when you walk the dog. Whatever routine you have can be adapted to enable you to invest in a younger believer. Ordinary moments used more intentionally can provide valuable time to share our lives with others.

Is there just one younger Christian in your life you could be investing in? How can you be intentional and get alongside her?

Once you have thought about who this younger Christian is, it's not a massive leap to think how you can be intentionally getting alongside her. If no one springs to mind, ask God. The truth is, we always make room for the things we really want to do.

So, where do you start when it comes to discipleship?

## Teach Biblical Truth

Do we challenge a younger Christian's addiction, theft, gossip, sexual immorality, idol of comfort or misuse of money? Honestly, it can feel daunting. We may feel out of our depth, but we need to trust God and his Word. Deepak Reju says,

*If you are a Christian who seeks to live faithfully and to live according to God's Word, you can help in most every situation. You can't necessarily fix the problem, but you can find ways to help them in their struggle... A centrepiece of this discipleship culture are the members teaching one another from God's Word with the goal of growing in personal holiness. You, as a member, are called to counsel the Word to one another. And whether you realise it or not, you are a soldier who sits on the front lines of the battle in this discipleship culture.*[4]

When we teach the whole counsel of God, it is his Word and the Holy Spirit who convicts those we are discipling. He picks the

4. Deepak Raju, BC Core Seminar: Congregational Counselling Session (Capitol Hill Baptist Church, Week 4, December 18, 2011), p. 2.

agenda and where you start. Trust him. In his infinite wisdom, God knows exactly where to prod and challenge. He knows exactly what area of life he wants to address and tackle first. We simply need to consistently teach the Word of God and who Jesus is.

## Life-on-Life Discipleship

Life-on-life discipleship isn't a set programme or an allocated hourly slot. Jesus focused his attention on the 12 disciples; he lived and ate with them. He didn't book individual one-to-one meetings once a fortnight with John or Peter. He walked and talked with them along the way. As I have previously said, this is the bit we struggle with, and it's not just because we are afraid people will see the reality of our messy lives. It is also because many of us just don't want to give up our 'me time'.

## Admit We All Need Help

New believers sometimes think mature Christians know everything and have it all sorted. We know that's not true, and we need to dispel this myth. We can do so by modelling godly behaviour amid trials so new believers know hard times come and see how to cope well in them.

I would like to caveat the above by saying we do need to be wise in what we share. We don't need to share with new believers the serious, intimate details of our lives which may overburden and crush them. Having said that, don't hear in this the perfect excuse to never share anything about yourself or your life. Discipleship isn't detached and it isn't a professional relationship where there are clear-cut boundaries. We must be involved and give of ourselves sacrificially.

## We Need to Get to the Heart of the Matter

As Christians, we often dance around an issue, never quite getting to the point or being clear. We can do this because we don't want to cause offence or embarrassment or upset anyone. But we need to love well enough to ask the hard, painful, challenging questions and not avoid them because it makes us uncomfortable.

## Speaking the Truth in Love

Speak well, wisely and out of love. If we truly love someone, we will gently tell them what they need to hear even though we know they won't like it (and maybe not like us for saying it).

For some, even when there is serious sin, all too often we can be fearful to challenge, either brushing over or even ignoring it because we don't want to lose a friend or be the bad guy. Here is an obvious illustration of what I mean: A lady from church plans to marry a guy who isn't a Christian. Her friends are worried in the background but never quite say anything to her directly. They don't know how to. Occasionally, they may throw an obscure comment in about being unequally yoked or pray about it openly. But no one actually sits down with her and has the hard but important conversation, questioning the relationship and sharing concerns and biblical truth about the reality of marrying a non-Christian. We need to tell her the whole truth, not leaving out the hard bits, because we love her enough to do it. After all, 'Wounds from a friend can be trusted, but an enemy multiplies kisses' (Prov. 27:6).

## Point to Christ and Pursue Righteousness

We often flee what we should pursue and pursue what we should flee. In our discipleship, we need to speak truth in love, encourage others to think through their actions and start to become more aware of sin. This isn't about speaking condemnation; instead, we are thinking through past actions, spotting the recurring themes and weaknesses, so new believers can be more prepared to do battle and fight temptation. We are teaching them to flee sin and run to Christ.

## Apply and Hold Accountable

Don't just leave it hanging – ask the question of how we can apply what we have just read or talked about in our lives. Then we need to hold them accountable! Ask them the next time you see them how they are getting on with X, Y and Z. Be persistent in following up.

## Be Patient

Let's not be discouraged when it comes to discipleship; change is often slow. We need to be patient. Sin is an ongoing battle in our own lives, and we can't expect it to be any different for those we disciple. As mature Christians, we need to continue to point them to Christ, patiently repeating truths they have heard before and reminding them who they are in Christ.

Doing this is repetitive. You may feel like you have said the same thing a hundred times. It's like banging your head off a brick wall. There may be times when you think they may walk away from God or doubt they are even saved.

Have you ever said to your kids, 'How many times do I have to tell you?' My son responded to this question once with 'I dunno, seven?' He wasn't being cheeky – he thought I was genuinely asking. How many times has God had to tell us? Seven? Seventy? Seventy times seven?

We need to patiently and lovingly persevere. Keep speaking truth, keep encouraging them onwards, keep pointing them to Christ and keep praying for and with them.

We have been doing accountability and discipleship at Niddrie for over 10 years, and nearly 90 per cent of our congregation has a one-to-one accountability partner in their life, discipling and mentoring them. There is no doubt it has had a significant impact for good on our congregation, complementing the work of our elders and ultimately serving the body.

## Further Resources:

- 20schemes' First Steps Series
- Susan Hunt, *Spiritual Mothering: The Titus 2 Model for Women Mentoring Women* (Crossway, 2016)
- Melissa Kruger, *Growing Together: Taking Mentoring beyond Small Talk and Prayer Requests* (Crossway, 2020)
- Edward Welch, *Side by Side: Walking with Others in Wisdom and Love* (Good News Publishers, 2015)

# 9

## Accountability

It's hard to separate discipleship and accountability. In one way, it's basically the same conversation using different words. At Niddrie we have evolved and developed new words such as one-anothering (two women of similar maturity supporting one another) and one-to-ones (one mature Christian mentoring someone younger in the faith). I'm not sure the terminology is that significant, but rolling it out in practice is.

You won't find the word accountability in your Bible concordance, but you will find the principles and examples immersed within the discipling relationships we see in Scripture.

The most obvious place to start would be with Jesus himself. He chose 12 disciples and did life with them. They ate together, travelled together, talked together and were taught by Jesus along the way (John 12:16; Mark 3:7, 20 and 6:1, 30–32). He taught them exactly who he was.

Jesus was intentional, investing his time and energy into the lives of the 12. I'm fairly sure they weren't the easiest bunch of blokes to love. We see scriptural evidence of squabbles, they were slow in understanding his teaching and all too often some were full of their own importance and agendas. From the hothead to the betrayer, different personalities mushed together in this group; yet Jesus was patient, loving and continued to teach.

Another example we see is Paul. He invested his time in Timothy and Titus, even calling them his 'true son' or 'my dear son' (1 Tim. 1:2; 2 Tim. 1:2; Tit. 1:4). He was their spiritual father and clearly had a genuine love and concern for them. Paul taught them the gospel and modelled godly living so they could be sent out to do the same. Ultimately, this should be our aim in our accountability relationships: we should desire to see people grow and eventually see them invest in someone else's life. I regularly ask my ministry women who they are being intentional with, investing in and reading the Bible with. There is always someone younger in the faith needing someone to point them to Christ.

I laid the foundations of accountability in the last chapter, and I don't want to repeat the same thing, but I do want to think through this topic a bit more practically.

Many women are frightened, even apologetic in their manner, when they ask someone if they would like to study the Bible and do accountability. We don't need to be afraid. You may be surprised by how many women are desperate to be asked. When we are talking about this with others, maybe we simply need to get over ourselves and step up. Worst case is they say no. After all this time at Niddrie, accountability is so imbedded within our culture it's the norm and expected. In fact, many new believers ask who their one-to-one is going to be. We don't have to chase them down or pursue them! They simply think this is the normal thing women do because they don't know any different. I find it sad it's not the normal way most Christians do life.

As I explained in chapter 2, Niddrie has a discipleship pathway, approved book list, and set questions. This makes discipleship easier as the mature Christian doesn't have to work out what to do, what book to use and so forth as all the foundational work has been done.

## The First One-To-One

For a first one-to-one I follow the same format every time, even if I have a pre-existing relationship with the person or we have already been studying the Bible together. I take the opportunity to explain the purpose of one-to-one and why it's good for us. I explain what confidentiality means (Niddrie has a policy outlining it) and talk through some examples of when I may have to share what she has told me with the elders. I explain that our elders don't need to know every detail of every conversation. However, if I'm concerned for her safety, the safety of others or if there is consistent, deliberate sinful behaviour and a refusal to repent then I will have no choice but to share this with the elders out of concern for her spiritual and physical wellbeing. Outlining our purpose and confidentiality statement doesn't prevent women from sharing but reminds them our elders care and confidentiality is taken seriously.

Then we work through the 17 questions below after I have explained their purpose and why they are asked. Mostly this is filled with much laughter, especially with the questions that are a bit more intimate. After going through all this, no one has ever said no and changed her mind about accountability, especially when I share my own personal struggle of first starting accountability. There isn't one person who isn't reluctant to share the blackness of their sinful heart with another – we all like our sin to stay hidden. But I, like all other women, have had to sit and decide for myself whether I want my character to grow as a Christian. It's hard to be vulnerable with someone else, to trust them and to share, but we must make a conscious choice to do it.

I explain I always like to work backwards and start at question 17, because by the time I get to question 1 the answer will be a real one rather than the standard, Of course God is the most important thing in my life. When we have sifted through all the questions, revealing the sinful responses and heart's desires at play, it's much harder to gloss over the most important question on the sheet with a trite answer.

## Niddrie Community Church's Accountability Questions

1. What has been more important to you than God in the last week?
2. Has your life displayed a love for Jesus and a joy because of Jesus this week?
3. What in the Bible this week has taught you, rebuked you, corrected you or trained you in righteousness?
4. Have you given yourself to deep, heartfelt prayer – adoring God, confessing sin, interceding for others?
5. Is there any sin that you have become aware of but love too much to repent of?
6. How have you responded when others have pointed out sin in your life?
7. When you have seen someone sin, have you humbly challenged them, or have you proudly gossiped about them?

8. Have you been deliberate in caring for and discipling your family this week?
9. Is your public life and devotion for Jesus a mirror of your private life and devotion to Jesus?
10. Have you been bold in sharing Jesus with others, or have you shied away from it?
11. Have you been deliberate about building relationships with those who don't know Jesus?
12. Have you been good and faithful with what God has given you in terms of time, money and gifts?
13. Is there anyone you need to forgive or seek forgiveness from?
14. Are you allowing bitterness to build up towards anyone?
15. Have you been with someone this week that could be misunderstood or deemed inappropriate?
16. Have there been times when you have lost self-control because of alcohol, drugs, anger or lust?
17. Has your use of social media – time spent on it and what you have posted on it – honoured Jesus this week?

The thing everyone asks is, 'Do I have to ask all the questions?', and the answer is always yes. We aren't God, so we don't know what's ruling someone's heart or how the Lord will prompt them. The questions help us to better understand the person. We can't assume; even when they look like adorable sweethearts there could be a whole sinful mess under the surface.

The basic outline of a one-to-one is catch up, study, questions and prayer. This usually takes me an hour and a half, but some manage it in an hour. There is no hard and fast rule about how long it should take. I don't systematically go through all the questions one by one each time we meet, but I do ask them all.

As you become more familiar with the questions and begin to know the other person better, it will become easier to ask the questions in normal conversation without it seeming contrived.

I always ask, 'What question don't you want me to ask?' And I usually finish by checking on whatever I was keeping them accountable for last time.

I don't take notes – not even for prayer – during our accountability. God is good because when it comes to pastoral stuff, I have the memory of an elephant, unlike everyday life when I can't hold a thought. However, there are some who take notes. I'm always a bit cautious about writing things down as notebooks can be lost and people who shouldn't see things may. If you are planning to take notes, I suggest you store it in line with your confidentiality policy and aim for vague highlights rather than detail.

No matter how much time I spend with someone outside of accountability, I always ensure we have a fixed, regularly scheduled formal time for accountability. Random conversations come up outside of scheduled times – and we can't say, 'No, we can't talk about this until Thursday at 1 p.m.' – but the regular slot gives it the importance it needs.

## Accountability in Action
Below are some pointers to think through for your own accountability meetings.

### *Before you start an accountability relationship, pray for the Lord's guiding.*
Who should you be discipling? Who should be discipling you? It isn't always helpful to meet with your best friend. You need

someone who is going to challenge you and someone you can learn and grow from. Make a wise choice.

### Decide times and topics.
Agree on how frequently you should meet and what you should study. If you're the one being discipled and struggling in a particular area, or would like to understand a subject better, let the person you are meeting with know.

### Be honest.
I know it seems an obvious thing to say, but we need to be honest and not hide behind unhelpful and confusing half-truths. It can take time for others to feel comfortable opening up to us (and vice versa). Be patient; it can take years to have upfront and honest conversations.

### Ask the dreaded questions.
At the time of writing this, 20schemes has seven church plants, and they don't all use the same set of questions. But they all use their own version consistently. I can't stress how important it is for a church to create their own elder-approved version and stick to it. Otherwise, what happens is aimless time spent talking about a load of rubbish.

### Avoid turning your time into spiritual-gossip sessions.
The purpose of you meeting together is to encourage, challenge and pray together. It is so tempting to get sucked into gossip, but we have to remember we aren't interested in what the neighbours have been saying or what was overheard in the coffee queue. Our focus is the other person's soul.

### *Be open to having partners you didn't expect.*

The right person for accountability isn't always who we think or want. The right person may not be our cup of tea or may even grate on us a little, but they may be the perfect choice for us. The relationship may challenge our sinfulness and help grow us. We may even end up really loving them in time. I always encourage women to give it a go for at least six months. If it truly isn't working after that, we would look to find an alternative. In the main, this six-month trial period works wonders and the women's fear and apprehension dissolves as they start to get to know each other.

### *Stick to the confidentiality policy.*

I have already talked about confidentiality, but it's important for me to come back to it. There will be times when someone says, 'Can I tell you something, but you can't tell anyone?' This might stroke our egos a little, but please don't agree to this. If they share something serious, you may have to tell the elders or authorities. Don't box yourself into a corner you can't get out of. More often than not, once a lady understands the confidentiality boundaries you are tied to, she will tell you anyway. Most churches have an active confidentiality policy and procedure the church members, volunteers and staff must adhere to. It's there for your protection as well as for the person sharing the secret.

## Accountability is at the Heart of All We Do

Accountability is one of the hardest and at times most painful things I have done, but it has been an absolute privilege to speak into the lives of young women. It's a joy to watch their faith and character grow. I have found it just as challenging to the soul as they do. As I challenge sin, I'm always questioning my own heart and asking myself if I struggle with this sin also. This has encouraged me to keep short accounts and be honest about the state of my own heart, driving me back to Christ and his Word. I always remind myself I have nothing but Christ to bring to the table and the encouragement to keep on keeping on. There are times when I'm asked a question I simply don't have an answer to. In these moments, I'm grateful for the men our elders are as they provide godly wisdom and direction.

Discipleship and accountability are at the heart of all we do in our women's ministry. These relationships fuel the events and socials we organise, not the other way around. What I mean is our events are driven by the discipleship relationship. I would venture to say almost all of women's ministry in the West is events driven. There seems to be an expectation that these seminars, workshops and courses will kick-start some sort of amazing discipleship and accountability movement within a congregation. But I'm not convinced it works that way. I'm not saying there have not been pockets of women moved by a seminar to start something meaningful, because I know it has happened. But, I actively challenge you to look at the evidence or results from these mass events. Women may be going home more theologically robust, but how many seriously take action and put what they have learnt into practice? How many women in a discipleship course invited a younger woman into their lives to actively disciple them 24/7 for the long haul? I would guess few have.

I'm passionate about discipleship and accountability because it's important. I remember as a young believer being told unhelpful rubbish about the Bible. I remember my friend

Marjory (an older, wiser Christian) patiently taking me to the Bible, debunking the nonsense and fluff, and pointing me to Christ. She invested in me and encouraged me too. Our relationship has changed over the years because I have grown and matured, but she is still in my life 30-plus years later.

As we approach accountability, may we keep Philippians 1:6 in our minds: 'being confident of this, that he who began a good work in you will carry it on to completion until the day of Christ Jesus'.

# 10

# Saved for a Purpose

*For we are his workmanship, created in Christ Jesus for good works, which God prepared beforehand, that we should walk in them. (Eph. 2:10, ESV)*

All Christians have been saved for a purpose and are called to acts of service. There aren't just five or six people in our congregations or care teams that are gifted for service and the rest simply bystanders. Yet this seems to be how a lot of churches operate. It may be people don't recognise their gifts, think their gifts are insignificant or perhaps think they don't need to serve because *you're* doing everything, or at least the six faithfuls are doing everything. But there may be someone in your congregation who is desperate to be given a chance, but there is no room or opportunity to learn.

Are you making room for others? Are you looking for them? To nurture a gift and help someone who is talented grow, you must first spot them and their talent!

We need to be vigilant, or, to use more Christian terminology, we need to spot potential gifting. They may not be the most obvious ones on the surface, but we need to think it through so we can invest in and nurture them, preparing and equipping them for service in our church plants and churches.

As we start thinking through how we grow and invest in the next generation of potential women's workers, pastoral care team members, mature Christians and active church members, we need a plan. This plan isn't miraculously going to create itself: we need to seriously look at how we serve and invest in people through discipleship, training and time.

I want to focus on three main areas to get the conversation started about how you can equip others: spotting, investing and enabling.

## Spotting Gifts

When it comes to identifying spiritual gifts, the usual way to do this is to hand out some sort of questionnaire and ask people to rank themselves on the 'giftometer'. I'm not saying this is a bad or unhelpful approach, but we need to do more than this for three simple reasons.

First, there are loads of people who are deluded about what they are good at. They think they can do something amazingly, but, to put it bluntly, they are actually not very good at it. How many times have we seen this on an *X-Factor* audition? People who think they have the x-factor bring a ton of swag to the audition but end up being hysterically bad. It's no different with spiritual gifts. Some people think they have a gift for preaching, teaching, hospitality or giving advice, but their gifts lie elsewhere.

Which brings me to my second issue: someone is telling them they are amazing. On these questionnaires there is always a section suggesting they seek advice from someone who knows them well and can comment on their gift set. This is a helpful step only if they actually ask someone who is spiritually mature and will love them enough to be honest with them. In my experience, Christians aren't the greatest when it comes to telling people what they don't want to hear. People don't like to burst bubbles or discourage. Few want to be seen as the bad guy.

Lastly, the ones who think they have no discernible gifts are usually the ones who have amazing gifts. So, my caution with the academic method of ranking your gifts on a form is simply that it may not give a clear picture. The forms are useful, but I would suggest caution when using this method in isolation.

The truth is, everyone is good at something, but they may just be focusing on the wrong thing. So here are some practical principles to keep in mind as you talent spot and look for giftedness.

### Engage your brain and pay attention.

I suppose the simplest way of thinking about spotting giftedness is to say that you won't spot the gift set of women if you aren't watching out for them. The Bible is very clear in 1 Corinthians 12:12–27 – churches are one body with many parts. We see that specifically in verse 12: 'Just as a body, though one, has many parts, but all its many parts form one body, so it is with Christ.' And again, in verse 27: 'You are the body of Christ, and each one of you is a part of it' (NIRV).

### Pay attention to the little things.

If you're paying attention you are more likely to find pre-existing skills, personal quirks and hobbies to put to good use. Of course, the obvious things everyone will think about are playing an instrument or singing, doing crafts for clubs and cooking skills for hospitality. These are great gifts to spot and use for the benefits of the congregation. But let's not stop there. We have to start thinking out of the box. With a little bit of invention, something that seems insignificant can be used greatly to serve the church.

Let me give you an example. There is a lady in our congregation who I'm going to call Olivia. We had three snapshot conversations over a long period of time that one day suddenly linked together in my head.

Chat 1: Olivia told me she was off to write snail mail to someone. She loved writing letters, and I was thinking to myself, *Who actually writes real letters these days?*

Chat 2: Olivia told me about an app where I could send picture postcards to my family with updates of my kids to help them feel involved, from a distance, as the kids grew up.

Chat 3: We talked about her writing schedule. Every week without fail she emails, writes or contacts someone consistently.

At this time, I had spotted a gap of care for our older church members who couldn't be consistent at church for various reasons. I would regularly spend time thinking how we could involve the wider church in getting regular updates to shut-ins. I was also thinking about ways I could encourage Olivia to actually engage with church members on a deeper level.

Two needs plus three pieces of random information, and I had this idea Olivia could start a postcard ministry. I asked Olivia to write to everyone on a short list with regular and consistent church updates. Over time I increased the names on her list. The next step was to invite her to meet some of these people in person. This way, I slowly introduced her to the wider church community one relationship at a time. Her quirky gifts, put to good use, serve the body.

We don't need to be geniuses or entrepreneurs but mindful and a bit inventive when it comes to looking for people's gifts. I could have phoned all the ladies on the list myself and updated them and that would have done the job. But even though this new method took so much longer to implement, it has had a wider impact on the congregation and Olivia herself.

What I want you to take away from this story is that a great women's worker is the one who facilitates the women in her congregation to serve each other rather than doing it all herself.

It's a massive mind shift to recognise one of your biggest roles is to prepare and equip, which takes much more time and investment than simply doing it yourself. It will benefit your congregations much more in the long run, leaving them stronger and less dependent on the few. And for those of you in church plants, I understand in the early days there are fewer bodies to share the roles, but it's helpful to have this in mind as you grow.

### Investing in a Few Gifted Women

Investing in gifted women has been harder at Niddrie as the congregation has grown. It is not possible to keep an eye on everyone and spot all the potential gifts. The way I have dealt with this over the years is simply to invest in a few at one time. This isn't that different an approach to what I used over a decade ago when I invested in the care team girls. The biggest difference is the size of group I can invest in has greatly diminished and I have to put in more effort. This year, for instance, I am being intentional with two women I have known for a while in our 20schemes' congregations. Even though I know them, I hope spending time with them more intentionally will help me recognise their gifts and encourage them to use them.

### *Put it to the test.*

We can learn much about potential gifting by watching how our congregation interacts: Who always steps up and serves before you ask, who shows initiative and fills the gap, who always spends time speaking to the old dears or chats to any newbies, and the list goes on. These little tell-tale signs can show the beginning of a gift set that could prove useful. When you spot something, put it to the test. Give them a little bit of responsibility, a task, to see if you're right and see if they step up. The more they step up the more responsibility we give.

### *Share responsibility.*

Make opportunities for sharing responsibilities with others in the congregation. We need to accept they probably will drop the ball at times, but the best lessons come from the mistakes we make. We must share responsibility with others, giving them room to grow and develop. Obviously, practise wisdom with how much responsibility you give them at one time. All too often we want to wait until we think they are ready to serve or meet some random idea of maturity. How are they ever going to be ready if you don't let them practise? Sadly, in many churches people from deprived areas often get sidelined with menial jobs and aren't offered the opportunity to serve in more responsible roles. I was talking about this at a conference, and one guy said, 'Surely you don't expect us to have *them* dealing with tasks such as the church finances.' My answer was simply, 'Yes, if they are saved, capable, qualified and mature enough, does it matter what side of the tracks they come from?'

## Enabling Women to Serve

About 95 per cent of the women I approached about serving had to be slowly encouraged into a role. Women you would look at now and think are amazing in their roles didn't achieve instant success. Rome wasn't built in a day; we will need patience as our ministry women take on their roles.

So, how can we enable people to serve?

### *Personal approach.*

Don't discount the personal approach. Emails requesting help or pointing out a need have their place. But people are more likely to serve and say yes if you take the time to personally approach them. Talk to them, hear their fears, encourage them, explain why you think they would be great and give them time to think about it. Problems can be worked around and fears can be allayed.

### *Help and support them out of their comfort zone.*

Sometimes people just need you to support them until they feel a bit more solid in the role. Being more hands-on in the beginning can be helpful.

### *One step at a time.*

It may be you see the potential in someone and can imagine them in a high responsibility role. Even if that is true and they are capable, sometimes telling someone your end goal can scare them off. It just seems too big, too overwhelming, too out of their reach at the beginning. Most women I have worked with and encouraged into key roles haven't started there but with a smaller, more manageable role. I have encouraged and trained them, progressing them slowly step by step into the envisaged role. I don't think this is deceitful, just more strategic.

## *Help them to fail well.*

I think this is one of the most important things I can say about enabling women to serve. The biggest fear many women have is simply making a mistake and failing. We need to create a climate where we help people to recover well from the mistakes they are inevitably going to make.

## Appendix Toolkit

- Appendix 4: Passing on the DNA.

# PART 3

*'If any of you lacks wisdom, you should ask God, who gives generously to all without finding fault, and it will be given to you' (Jas. 1:5).*

# 11

---

# When You Don't Agree with Leadership Decisions

As we enter the last portion of the book, I want the pace to change. Many of these chapters will be short and punchy. They will focus on those questions we never want to give voice to, but we must. Pretending there isn't an issue won't make it go away, and, left unaddressed, doing so may eventually turn into sinful thoughts and bitterness.

This is one of these topics. My elders are good, godly, wise men, but they aren't infallible. Neither am I. There have been times when the elders have made a ministry decision, and I simply didn't agree with it. Worse yet, I may have actually flagged a problem or risk, but they still went ahead. This chapter isn't about how to get your elders to listen to you or to make better decisions but to encourage us to look at our own sinful hearts. Check the root of the problem and deal with it.

## The Root of the Problem

In the early days I struggled with this, for a lot of reasons, but at the heart of the matter was my arrogant pride. I'm a control freak, and during that time I lacked trust. It's as simple as that. Now I could tie this up in a nice, sweet bow, but as a women's worker and a church member I am called to submit to the authority over me and to do so well. Submitting well means we are not to complain, pout, have a tantrum, try to manipulate, write some passive-aggressive email, make pointed comments or constantly repeat the opinion like a mantra because we think no one is listening (they are listening, they just don't agree with us). In other words, nagging like a dripping tap. Our elders give weight to our opinions and listen to what we have to say. Sometimes this may alter the decision and change their thinking, but other times it doesn't. I try to share my opinion once and leave it. This was probably one of the hardest things to learn. But in doing so, I ensure my voice is heard, and then I encourage myself to resist the temptation and trust. I try never to say, I knew it, or, I told you so.

There are times, for example, when we have been in an interview and the candidate is a risk. We have recognised their strengths and weaknesses and know there are certain personality quirks that could frustrate the congregation. This happened once with one of our male interns. He had very fixed opinions about women in authority and wouldn't even consider reading a commentary written by a woman. We knew and discussed the risks. I voted no. His internship was difficult and many of the women on the team and in our congregation struggled with and were hurt by his attitude and actions. He did damage (temporarily). Now, I don't want to get into any real detail about the situation. I do want to make it clear that he was a man of God who truly felt his interpretation of Scripture was correct and was trying to be faithful and have integrity to the Word. We were never going to agree on scriptural interpretation, but that wasn't what I was asked to do. My role was to be a godly woman, submitting well to the authority of the elders' decision to employ him and caring for the women struggling in the background.

This was a hard period. At times it felt like we had gone backwards in time by 20 or more years. I had to remind the ladies around me that our elders cared for and heard us and our voice was important to them. I reminded them (and myself) that we needed to trust them. We were a teaching church, and this was part of the process, but that didn't make it feel any better. We had to check our hearts and make sure we ran to God with our sin instead of stirring up discontent.

## Responding Well

In these types of situations, the only thing we can control is how we respond, and we need to set an example of being godly, faith-filled women. I believe we need to be wise in any ministry role, as the eyes of our congregation are looking at how we respond in these situations; some may even take their lead from us.

When difficult moments like this come up for you, ask yourself these questions:

1. What is it you want in this situation that you aren't getting?
2. What is ruling your heart when you won't submit? How do you respond?
3. What kind of example are you being to the wider church?
4. What sin is driving your attitude and causing division,

discontentment or anger? What sinfulness do you need to repent from?

5. How can you respond better the next time? What needs to change?

At the core of this chapter is one take-home grain of truth. As the only thing we can control is how we respond, make sure you check your heart and respond well. There are always going to be moments when you simply don't agree with leadership decisions; make sure your response to that isn't sinful. Unless your elders and leaders are going against the Word of God in preaching and encouraging heresy, make sure you speak wisely and submit and respond in a way that brings honour to God and doesn't damage the body. Turn to God, pray and ask for his help to respond well. Pray for your elders, as well. The longer I am in ministry the more I realise the heavy weight and responsibility these men carry as they care for their congregations.

We are called to trust and obey the Word of God. He is very clear.

*Have confidence in your leaders and submit to their authority, because they keep watch over you as those who must give an account. Do this so that their work will be a joy, not a burden, for that would be of no benefit to you.*
*Pray for us. We are sure that we have a clear conscience and desire to live honourably in every way. I particularly urge you to pray so that I may be restored to you soon. (Heb. 13:17–19)*

# 12

# When Men Won't Step Up

What do you do when a man won't step up? I have been asked this question, in its many forms, over the last 10 years. This question has two different scenarios: home and ministry. Is it a different question? I don't know that it is. The biblical truth and principles are the same.

## Home

Many times women tell me they want their husbands to step up, but they don't. These women are frustrated and don't know what to do, so how do we tackle this as women's workers without undermining or usurping the biblical framework for leadership in our home and church? How can we counsel well in this situation?

## Ministry

I believe the Bible is clear: as women we don't have to submit to *all* men, only husbands and elders. Yet, there are times in ministry when we must submit to the ministry team leader (who is perhaps male). We are always teaching at 20schemes, trying to help our ministry men learn their roles and hone their gifts. In those cases, many times interns have been given a trainee leadership position in a specific area of ministry that they have to learn to lead and direct. In your role there will be men in positions of leadership to whom you will have to submit. Just as a wife shouldn't undermine or usurp the biblical authority over her, neither should the women's worker.

I want to start by thinking through this subject from two primary perspectives: personally (how this applies to our life) and pastorally (how this applies to the women in our care).

## Why Don't Men Lead?

Let's take a few minutes to think through some of the reasons why a man might not want to lead.

1. Maybe he doesn't know how to lead. Perhaps they haven't had leadership exampled to them, and they don't know where to start. It's not like they suddenly wake up one morning and instantly are the most gracious yet direct leader alive.

2. Maybe he thinks he is leading and doesn't even realise he is not.

3. Maybe he is lazy and can't be bothered to step up. It might be he is one of those Peter Pan men who has simply traded the mum who did everything for him for a wife. He would rather play videogames or watch football than take any responsibility.

4. Maybe he is just the laid-back or the easy-going type and taking the lead doesn't come naturally to him.

5. Maybe he has tried but has given up. This is hard for us to

admit to ourselves, but it could be that he has tried, and it has gone horrifically wrong. He has been discouraged and even had his confidence beaten down by those around him. Now he is apprehensive to take the lead and thinks it's easier to keep the peace rather than try again.

6. Maybe he doesn't lead because he knows it will be a battle. He has tried to lead in the past, and, when he tries, there is a massive argument and battles which end in tears and tantrums.

## Do We Let Them Lead?

It is true there are many reasons why men won't lead. The list is way more extensive than my six points. But it is also true there are men who want to lead and step up, but women won't let them.

When it comes to male leadership, all too often what I *hear* is, 'I'm struggling because I want my husband to lead me and he won't. He leaves everything up to me to decide.' But sadly, what I *see* is a man struggling to lead a wife who doesn't want to be led. It doesn't happen only to wives and husbands. Many of our women at church struggle to submit to the leadership when they don't like what they are hearing or are being asked to do. On the surface some may look, talk and act like godly, mature women, but there is carnage and war behind the scenes as they vie for the top-dog position. Living like this can be a bit like a master strategy game, but unfortunately without any real winners.

What about if men don't lead well? Do we still have to let them lead? I would have to say it is a slightly different situation for a wife versus a single woman. I believe you have a responsibility to submit biblically and be led, even though men aren't perfect and will, like the rest of the human race, make mistakes. These men have been appointed and given a responsibility to lead us and will be held to account before God for how they do so. However, if you are asked to do something contrary to God's Word, I want to stress that first and foremost we must submit primarily to God and obey his Word. I just want to concisely say that I think it is a completely different conversation when a husband or leader is physically or emotionally abusive, oppressively demanding obedience of his every word. Abuse in the guise of male leadership isn't acceptable in any way.

## How Should We Respond?

The temptation in this chapter is simply to focus on biblical submission and look at 1 Peter for some insight. Instead I want to focus on Judges 4, where we see a practical example of submitting when a man isn't quite stepping up to the mark.

*Now Deborah, a prophet, the wife of Lappidoth, was leading Israel at that time. She held court under the Palm of Deborah between Ramah and Bethel in the hill country of Ephraim, and the Israelites went up to her to have their disputes decided. She sent for Barak son of Abinoam from Kedesh in Naphtali and said to him, 'The LORD, the God of Israel, commands you: "Go, take with you ten thousand men of Naphtali and Zebulun and lead them up to Mount Tabor. I will lead Sisera, the commander of Jabin's army, with his chariots and his troops to the Kishon River and give him into your hands."'*
*Barak said to her, 'If you go with me, I will go; but if you don't go with me, I won't go.'*

*'Certainly I will go with you,' said Deborah. 'But because of the course you are taking, the honour will not be yours, for the Lord will deliver Sisera into the hands of a woman.' So Deborah went with Barak to Kedesh. (Judg. 4:4–9)*

I don't want to get into the minutiae of the text, but let's look at a general, overarching application of what we have been talking about. In particular, I want to focus on Deborah's response. I also want to be clear Barak does not hold a position of authority over Deborah, and, because of this, in many ways this isn't an ideal example. To be honest, it has proven difficult to find an ideal example of this complex situation. I feel it is helpful to look at Deborah and how she responds to Barak when he clearly doesn't want to take on the leadership role God has given him to do.

In verse 6 we see Barak commissioned by the Lord to take on Sisera. Don't be fooled – Barak isn't a wimp or even someone who can't lead. He may not be a professional soldier, but he has an army of 10,000 fighting men under his command. I don't want you to think I am bashing Barak; he is, after all, listed in the heroes of the faith in Hebrews 11. But when he is commissioned by God he is reluctant to step up.

In his book on Judges, Barry Webb comments on Barak's actions:

*Does he have faith strong enough to go forward against overwhelming odds with nothing but a promise of God to rely on?... Barak's response to Deborah's command is neither a definite yes nor a definite no.*[1]

---

1. Barry Webb, *Judges and Ruth: God in Chaos,* Preaching the Word Commentary (Crossway, 2015), p. 97.

Barak isn't saying, 'Here I am Lord, ready and willing.' He is a bit more Gideon-esque in his approach to leadership at this moment. As with Gideon, the foe Barak faced was large, fierce and intimidating. In the cold light of day, perhaps his reticence is somewhat understandable. Deborah's response to him is immediate as she simply says, 'Certainly I will go' (v. 9).

Webb says of Barak,

*It could be seen as an act of piety in Barak's part. Barak has such a huge regard for Deborah as God's spokesperson that he wants her at his side so that he can always be directed by God's word through her...Clearly though, Deborah herself does not think this is how things should have been. For her, Barak's equivocation did not reflect well on him.*[2]

There is no doubt Deborah has issues with Barak's response. We see that in her response in verse 9: 'But because of the course you are taking, the honour will not be yours...' Deborah doesn't give him a hard time, nag him or force him to step up; she doesn't undermine him when she could so easily have done so or even give him a piece of her mind, tearing a strip off him. Deborah, however, does rebuke Barak about his course of action as she respectfully and truthfully shares the consequences of it. I think what she is doing is showing motherly concern for Barak. She is trying to love him well, encouraging him to rely solely on and trust in the Lord. Even then Barak could have changed his strategy, but he didn't. Deborah doesn't say any more – she simply does what Barak has asked of her.

---

2. Ibid. p. 97.

Deborah is a strong, gifted, capable woman who could have handled this in many ways, but in her we see an example. She clearly didn't think Barak was doing things the right way; nevertheless, she did as he asked. She, just as Barak did, made a choice.

We may think when a man won't lead there is nothing for us to do but take over and do it ourselves. But that would be acting like Barak by taking the wrong approach. We must choose to submit to God, example Christ in our lives, love and humbly serve those God has entrusted to lead us, and allow them to lead us.

So, what do you do when men won't lead?

- Pray. Pray God will give the men who lead us the wisdom, desire and gifts to step up and serve. Also pray we will love, submit and serve humbly.
- Speak to them in humility and love. There might be many reasons why he isn't stepping up, and it may be helpful to have a constructive and gentle conversation. This shouldn't be about nagging and taking cheap shots. By talking about the situation, we may be able to help or understand better their struggles.
- Seek accountability for your own attitude. Anger, disrespect, discontentment, pride and control issues – to name but a few – are the sinful attitudes that might be at play. When our sinful-self rules, we end up reflecting us and not Christ.
- Meet your own responsibilities. Be mindful of your own spiritual walk and do your own job to the best of your abilities.
- Ask help from the right people. This shouldn't be something you gossip about with your colleagues or friends. Be wise: talk to the right people.

There may be a point when you have done everything that has been asked, and you still need some help. When do you speak to the elders? Does that undermine the husband or ministry leader? It's not as easy to answer as you may think; nothing ever is. The trouble is, no situation is the same. We want to offer help without interfering or undermining.

What I do know clearly is we must go to the elders if we feel a woman is in danger from an oppressive and abusive husband or leader, if she is in some way facing harm or if there is deep-rooted, deliberate, unrepentant or ongoing sin. These are rare situations, and it would be helpful to sit down with your pastor and elders to work out what parameters and pastoral framework they want you to work within.

Practical examples in the Bible of when a woman has stepped out of the normal biblical pattern are few and far between (see Abigail's response in 1 Samuel 25). They are rare and unique, and this should tell us something in itself.

In the main, however, for women who are struggling with a man who is struggling to lead, I would encourage them to be gracious. In love, be patient with them, trusting the Lord. We all take time to grow and change. Let's encourage women to treat others with the grace and love the Lord has bestowed upon us.

## Further Resources

- Derek Cleave, *1 Peter,* Focus on the Bible (Christian Focus, 1999)
- Edmund Clowney, *The Message of 1 Peter*, The Bible Speaks Today (InterVarsity Press, 1988)
- David Helm, *1 & 2 Peter and Jude: Sharing Christ's Sufferings*, Preaching the Word Commentary (Crossway, 2008)

- John Piper, 'What Should a Wife Do When Her Husband Doesn't Lead Spiritually?', *Desiring God,* www.desiringgod.org/interviews/what-should-a-wife-do-when-her-husband-doesnt-lead-spiritually

- Barry Webb, *Judges and Ruth: God in Chaos*, Preaching the Word Commentary (Crossway, 2015)

# 13

# Dealing with Others' Expectations

In our sinfulness we twist everything, and being in ministry doesn't somehow make us superhumans. Christians are not immune to such things. One area I think everyone struggles with is dealing with other people's expectations. When we are in ministry, we may especially struggle in this regard since our funding comes from others' generous donations. However, the more I think about this the more I realise that at the heart of it is our fear of man. But we are called to serve without other people's expectations (good or bad) impacting us and what we do.

Fear of man, in a nutshell, is when we replace the fear of the Lord with the fear of people. Instead of God ruling our lives, we are ruled by people. Fear of man has many other names: peer pressure, people pleasing, or, for those who like the fancy counselling words, codependent. But whatever we call it, at the heart of it people matter more to us than God: 'Fear of man will prove to be a snare, but whoever trusts in the Lord is kept safe' (Prov. 29:25).

This might be something that rules our lives massively, and we are completely controlled by it all the time to where it affects our everyday lives. For others, we are sitting there smugly thinking to ourselves that this isn't an issue we need to pay much attention to. We say, 'I don't care what people think about me.' But the truth is that for all of us, at some point in our lives, fear of man plays a part. In the book *When People Are Big and God Is Small*, Ed Welch says the 'Fear of man is such a part of our human fabric that we should check for a pulse if someone denies it.'[1]

In the same book Ed Welch has a list of questions he uses to highlight the symptoms of the fear of man. I'm going to use my version of these questions.[2]

- Have you ever struggled with peer pressure? Do you care too much about what people think about you?
- Are you overcommitted? Are you one of those people who find it hard to say no even when you know wisdom tells you that you should?
- Do you feel you need respect from people?
- Do you think low self-esteem or worrying about others' opinions is a recurring theme for you?
- Do you feel like you're pretending to be something/ someone you're not?
- Are you always second-guessing decisions because of what other people might think?
- Are you afraid of making mistakes that will make you look bad in other people's eyes?

1. Edward Welch, *When People Are Big and God Is Small: Overcoming Peer Pressure, Codependency, and the Fear of Man* (P&R Publishing, 2012), p. 17.
2. Ibid. pp. 14–16.

- Is your private life different to your public life?
- Do you ever lie (think especially of little white lies) to people to cover up something silly, to be funny or even to make yourself look better?
- Do you avoid people, especially when you think you have said something, done something or think they think something weird about you?
- Do you compare yourself to other people?
- Have you ever been too scared to share your faith because others might think you are a complete numpty?

How did you fare? These exploring questions give a hint of how fear of man is playing out in our life.

## Who Is Controlling Us?

We fear people because they can expose and humiliate us; they can reject, ridicule or despise us; and they can attack, oppress and threaten us.

At the heart of these reasons is simply that we see people as bigger – more powerful and significant – than God. It's like we give other people the right and control to tell us what to feel, think and do.

Many of us crave the approval of other people or we fear their rejection. We feel that we *need* the acceptance of others, so we are controlled by that desire. When we start to think about this in more detail, more often it is a particular individual or type of person we crave approval from: parents, friends, our spouse, the pastor, the person in power, etc. We would not say it straight out, but our behaviour and language talks about needing and wanting something from them, such as their love, respect, approval, praise or acceptance. When we fear other people, we act in whatever way we think will enable us to gain their approval or avoid their rejection. When we are ruled by other people we make them our god and saviour.

The underlying idol, however, is self. When we crave approval and affirmation from other people, we, in effect, want them to worship us. We must ask ourselves whose agenda is ruling in our relationships: God's agenda or the self agenda. In those relationships where fear of man reigns, it will be evident our self-interest (self) is what rules us and that we want worship.

Are we beginning to recognise the influence of fear of man in our lives?

## Overcoming the Fear of Man

Our culture attempts to overcome the fear of man by boosting our self-esteem. You just need to read the magazines with the top 10 tips to improve your self-esteem or look at the giant row of self-help books in the library to see that. But our culture's solution only compounds the problem; it's simply a fancy way of us being more me-centred. The only thing that will truly liberate us from the fear of man is to turn away from me-centric thinking and become more God-centred; in other words, we need the fear of God. We need a big view of God. To fear God is to respect, worship, trust and submit to God.

The writer of Hebrews says we can approach God with confidence because of the work of Jesus our High Priest (Heb. 4:14–16). But the writer of Hebrews also says our God is a consuming fire whom we must worship with reverence and awe (Heb. 12:28–29).

When people are controlled by the expectations of others, we need to teach them the fear of the LORD. Encourage them to meditate on God's glory, greatness, holiness, power, splendour, beauty, grace, mercy and love. Encourage them to compare the person they fear with God.

### Check your heart

Examine what's at the heart of the matter. Try asking my favourite question, 'What is it I want here that I'm not getting?' What we are doing is examining what is at the heart of the fear that is driving our need. In recognising that it should drive us back to God.

We are not free to love other people when we fear their rejection or crave their approval. We may speak of loving someone, but in reality we are using them to gain the affirmation we crave. We may serve them, but we are actually serving our need for affirmation. If they do not deliver that affirmation, then we respond with bitterness, depression or anger. Or we often fear other people because we fear exposure. We wear a mask to prevent people from discovering the real us.

In God we have someone who knows us completely in all our need and sin. Yet still he accepts us and loves us. Confidence in the grace of God means we need not fear exposure, so we do not have to pretend with him.

When we recognise the true extent of our hearts, we need to run to God.

### Run to God

Seek forgiveness and rejoice that God forgives sin. Not only does he do that, but he also will help you resist the temptation in your life again. He protects and loves, and he is merciful to us. With God's help we can be truly transformed.

Understand and grow in the fear of the Lord. Remember who this life is all about, and dwell on him.

As we become more Christ-like, that perceived *need* we have for self-worship and affirmation from others decreases. Instead of our lives being about self, we find we love others more as our focus moves from self to God. Our lives will be transformed from self-service to serving God: 'You, my brothers and sisters, were called to be free. But do not use your freedom to indulge the flesh; rather, serve one another humbly in love' (Gal. 5:13).

If you don't get a handle on this idol, then your fear of man will continue to grow bigger, becoming more deeply imbedded in your life. Unless you run to Christ in repentance and prayer people will always matter more to you than God. If I leave you with the first question from the accountability list in chapter 9, What has been more important to you than God this week?, what would be your honest answer? The standard answer for most of us is 'God is the most important thing.' Truth is, a lot of the time we are lying; we all struggle with idols dethroning God and replacing him. Fear of man is a common one we all battle with in some way. Don't battle alone. We cannot allow fear of man to rule us; we need to run to God, repent, rely on him and ask him to help us deal with this crippling idol.

# 14

## Leadership Is Isolating

'You've been invited to come to the meeting.' I was gutted. The girls and I had planned to go out for dinner, and I had been really looking forward to it. What happened next was what I can only describe as *the* worst meeting I have ever been to. To top it off, yet again, I was the only female in the room. I sat feeling isolated and intimidated, speaking only when directly asked a question and then being as concise as possible. I listened intently as some guy was making a point, probably a very valid one, about the cultural demographic represented at the meeting. I looked around the room at this point and thought to myself, 'I think you'll find in this room *I'm* the minority, and my voice needs to be diluted by other women being present too.' To my horror I actually said this out loud, well, to my shame, a feistier version of it.

Being the only girl in the room is always isolating. Thankfully over time my voice has been diluted by others more eloquent than mine. But don't be fooled; in ministry it's not only these types of moments where you will, as a women's worker, feel alone and isolated. Being in leadership is isolating. Not only do you have to make the hard decisions and hear things you can't unhear, but all too often people are standoffish because they are wary.

Loneliness and isolation are demoralising, and few people really talk about it. When you are part of a church-planting or revitalising team, you often will be grafting away on your own for years with little or no help.

When we first launched 20schemes and Mez and I would travel to meetings all over Scotland, we met all these people slogging away on their own. I always felt sorry for them and wanted to help. I remembered how hard the early years were, and at least in our situations we had a small team. It's one of the main reasons I asked Rachel Williamson to write the chapter 'No One Else Is Coming' in *Unexceptional* (a book focusing on the experiences of women's workers in various contexts). Here is an excerpt of her church-planting experience:

> *Everything fell to me and Ian...We were desperate to have a team of people to help us. The magnitude of everyone coming to us was a huge strain. We had created a church that was 24/7. We were opening our house up around the clock; we were having people stay over, with our children giving up their beds; and someone was having tea with us every night. It was exactly how we had wanted it to be, but we didn't want and had never envisaged it being just us doing everything ourselves.* [1]

---

1. Rachel Williamson, 'No One Else is Coming' in Sharon Dickens, *Unexceptional* (10Publishing, 2019), p. 138.

For me to simply say, 'You're going to be isolated, so be prepared, suck it up and get over yourself', is not exactly the best or gentlest of pastoral approaches to take, no matter how true the words may be. If someone said that to me, I would have cried whilst resisting the temptation to kick them in the shins. I would love to be able to say this as gently as possible and with a ton of love and compassion, but there are times when you will absolutely feel lonely and on your own. Even with a team around you there will be moments like Rachel's, and all I have to offer is three thoughts: find people you can trust, rest well and trust God. I know this is not mind-blowing information, but it's still true.

## Find Godly People You Can Trust

At the worst moments in ministry – when I have had truly enough and questioned whether I can continue – someone has turned up at my door to encourage me to keep on. Many times that someone has been Miriam McConnell, thankfully with a tub of ice cream, a movie and a bag of sweets with her. We all know it's nothing to do with the ice cream, but everything to do with Miriam caring enough to come.

I urge you to pray for and find godly, mature people who you can trust. They should be from inside and outside your community. I have four women in my life to whom I would absolutely, no-holds-barred, dish up the personal dirt and be totally honest with. I genuinely can't tell you how freeing that is. These are safe and godly women who will listen, love me the same (no matter what I say) and point me to Christ. I haven't always had these four women in my life. The friendships have grown over time and with prayer. I pray these four will increase, as I meet more like-minded, safe and godly women. There are times when you just meet the right person at the right time, but there are other times when we must prayerfully seek support.

A word of warning though: 'safe' is the operative word. Sometimes all that glitters isn't gold. Sadly, when you are in leadership there are people who want to be your friend because they have their own agenda. Friendship is always going to be difficult to navigate when you are in pastoral ministry. There will always be things you can't share or tell people because of confidentiality. A true safe friend won't be concerned about what you can't share but will listen to what you can. Pick wisely.

## Rest Well

In the early days of ministry I really struggled to rest well. I had some twisted thinking going on about people in the congregation paying my wages and that it was unfair for me to take time off. It wasn't helpful thinking, and a few times when I was seriously overstretched and overwhelmed my pastor had to step in and make me take time off – even then I struggled to stop and rest. My thinking was being fuelled by my fear of man, and I had to address it and learn to stop before I crashed and burned.

After serving at church for 10 years, I was given the privilege of a sabbatical. Since I'm not great at taking time off and don't find it that restful when I do, I asked the elders if I could take my sabbatical a bit differently. I wanted to take an art class one morning a week, and to my absolute surprise they said yes. When I'm painting, I totally switch off. Each week I would paint, and my brain would be so engrossed it wouldn't think of anything else. That was restful.

Whatever your thing is, find it and use it. Some people like climbing mountains, swimming in the sea, going to the gym, running a marathon or baking cakes. We all have something we find restful. It's so easy when you are the only one on the ground to feel guilty or feel like you can't leave the community in case something happens. We must give ourselves permission to turn the phone off and rest. Not only do we have to rest well physically, but we also must make sure we have a proper Sabbath, resting spiritually. This isn't an indulgence, it's a necessity and a command: 'Six days you shall labour, but on the seventh day you shall rest; even during the ploughing season and harvest you must rest' (Ex. 34:21).

Today I was with one of our women's workers, encouraging her to make regular and planned time in her schedule to prayerfully retreat with God. In the early days, Miriam and I would do this monthly – hanging out and praying for the other women on the care team. These days, it isn't that regular, but I still spend planned, focused time on ministry reflection and resting in God.

Find out what really refreshes you physically and spiritually and then intentionally schedule it in and make it a priority. When you do, guard that time (but not legalistically – serious crisis doesn't plan itself around your schedule).

## You Are Never Really Alone

I know it seems obvious, but sometimes I think we need to state the obvious: even when you feel alone you are never really on your own. Christ is with you. He is the only 100 per cent trustworthy, completely safe, totally wise one you can talk to and at any time.

*...for I have learned to be content whatever the circumstances. I know what it is to be in need, and I know what it is to have plenty. I have learned the secret of being content in any and every situation, whether well fed or hungry, whether living in plenty or in want. I can do all this through him who gives me strength. Yet it was good of you to share in my troubles... And my God will meet all your needs according to the riches of his glory in Christ Jesus. (Phil. 4:11–14, 19)*

It's all too easy in ministry to become self-reliant, ploughing on in your own strength. It's all too easy to spend time studying the Word without dwelling on it and spending meaningful time with God. We must remind ourselves regularly on whom we need to rely. Pray, cry and cling to him; lean and rely on him; trust and worship him; dwell in him. He is not all you have but *all* you need.

# Afterword

When we were going through the editing process my editor suggested concluding remarks, but she probably didn't expect me to admit to this on paper. The editing process is weird, but good for your soul. After pouring yourself onto the pages they chop, challenge and question, as well as fix your grammar (thankfully!). There's a point when you start to question your own voice. Looking back and reflecting on the past 15 years as I've been writing this book, I see the women's work I do now is a bit like the finished edited copy of a book. I started with a ministry plan in mind of what it should look like but as people have challenged my thinking, chopped things that haven't worked and completely fixed the things I was doing wrong, much like in the editing process – it has all been for the better.

So, I leave you with the same challenge my pastor Mez McConnell gave me when I wanted to dodge the women's ministry bullet and opt for the less messy and easier route of service. "Pray for a vision for women's ministry and come up with a plan."

Let's see what God will do.

# APPENDICES

# APPENDIX 1:

# Women's Ministry Plan Outline

If you have more than one ministry, identify each individual one and either work through the questions and process for each or ask the person leading a specific ministry to follow the same process and collate the information for analysis. This will help you to keep a note of progress for each ministry for an annual review which will enable you to plan for the following year.

Note: It's hard to be objective when you oversee a specific ministry. All too often leaders see the review as a personal reflection of their leadership. Cultivate a culture where review is normal and encourage others to see that their ministry is not who they are. If something isn't working it doesn't mean they have personally failed; it simply means the ministry isn't working.

Establish from the start the following:

1. What is your vision for the women's ministry in one sentence?

2. What are your ministry goals and aims? Identify ministry goals and aims for year one, three and five.
3. Where are you currently in the ministry process?
4. How are you practically going to achieve your vision and goals for the current year, year three and year five? What will be your strategy to achieve this?

Your aims and goals may change over time. Just because you have a plan for year three doesn't mean you have to stick to it. The ministry may have evolved or opened up in an unexpected area. This is why annual reviews are helpful and tweaking the plan is essential. It's helpful to know what direction you are heading in, but it's a map that can be altered. Make sure you hold to your plan with a light grip – be flexible.

## Define Your Ministry

You don't have to answer each question listed here, but these are the kinds of questions you are unpacking in this step. This section of your plan should be between a half page to a page long.

- Why does this ministry exist?
- How does this ministry fit into the overall vision for the church?
- What is the biblical basis for this ministry?
- What is Scripture calling us to in this ministry?
- What are you attempting to accomplish in this ministry?

## Describe the Present

Be honest and consider what the ministry looks like today. What does it consist of? List numbers, programmes, leaders, etc. Be thorough and detailed in your description. Make this at least one page long.

## Diagnose Current Problems

What are the current problems in this ministry? What is holding the ministry back? (*I realise this may be uncomfortable. Remember this evaluation shouldn't come from a place of self-righteousness or pride; rather, humbly consider the reality of what is going on.*)

- What is frustrating?
- What are we missing or lacking in the ministry?
- What obstacles are we facing?

For the best results, you need to be thorough and honest. List all the obstacles that come to mind.

You don't have to answer just these questions. There may be others more appropriate for your specific context. Consider and add any others to the list, adapting this resource to match your need.

## Design a Plan

Once you have identified need and obstacles, start to construct the plan for year one, three and five.

- What is required to solve the above identified problems?
- What is required to move the ministry forward?
- What specific things are you going to start, stop or do to move forward?
- What are you going to do to move beyond the present?
- What will we accomplish this year to move the ministry forward for the year three and five goals?

I find it helpful to have a timeline and plan. I hold this loosely by which I mean I don't legalistically drag people over the target dates. However, it is helpful to have a realistic map to ensure you can plan, best use resources and keep the ministry heading in the right direction. It's so easy to slip into the habit of delivering the service and forget the whole point of the ministry. For example, if the aim of an activity is not clearly driving the ministry then activities such as craft groups can easily become more about the technique than gospel opportunity. People might go home with amazing Christmas cards without hearing the true Christmas story.

Make specific and measurable goals in this section. Don't feel like you must answer all the above questions, but it is helpful to try and tackle them all.

Write what you are going to do in the coming year. Make sure to keep your goals specific and measurable.

## Detail the Progress

This step is not an afterthought but is critical to the whole process. How will we implement our plan over the coming year? In detailing the progress, your headings in this section should be months (January, February, March…). Underneath each month, list what goals (from step 4 above) you will accomplish in that month.

## Plan Your Development

It's so easy to simply focus on the ministry without considering self or your care team. Ask yourself what is your plan for personal growth this year? What are you going to read, study or do to grow?

---

# Evaluating Members' Gifting Toolkit

When considering who can serve in what capacity, loving, honest evaluation is a good place to start. This activity is designed to help identify and evaluate the gift base you have available. Think of it like a stock take. Evaluations enable you to think through how you could invest in or train them, thus enabling them to serve more. Think about the top 10 women you spend most of your time with, or your Bible study group, core group, etc. Rate each woman from 1 (very poor) to 5 (amazing) in each of the categories in the table on the next page.

|   | Name | Evangelism | Bible Study | Sunday Service |
|---|------|------------|-------------|----------------|
| 1 |      |            |             |                |
| 2 |      |            |             |                |
| 3 |      |            |             |                |
| 4 |      |            |             |                |
| 5 |      |            |             |                |
| 6 |      |            |             |                |
| 7 |      |            |             |                |
| 8 |      |            |             |                |
| 9 |      |            |             |                |
| 10 |     |            |             |                |

# Evaluating Members' Gifting Toolkit

| One-to-One | People | Service | Personal Relationships | Other Area Distinctive to Your Setting? |
|---|---|---|---|---|
|  |  |  |  |  |
|  |  |  |  |  |
|  |  |  |  |  |
|  |  |  |  |  |
|  |  |  |  |  |
|  |  |  |  |  |
|  |  |  |  |  |
|  |  |  |  |  |
|  |  |  |  |  |
|  |  |  |  |  |

Evangelism: How good are they at getting alongside non-believers, bringing them to events and church or studying the Bible with them?

Bible Study: This is not just about attendance but how much they take part in the discussion, how helpful their contribution is, participation in prayer and how they interact with the other girls.

Sunday Service: This is not just how they serve, but how are they interacting with the other congregational members? Are they spending time visiting with just their circle or are they working the room? Are they helpful and welcoming to new people? Is it all about them and how the church serves them?

One-to-one: Do they have a one-to-one? If so, are they growing? Do they only receive or are they also getting alongside younger believers?

People: Can they see the bigger gospel picture when it comes to people or is it always about themselves and ensuring they get equality? Do they visit some of the more obscure, elderly or vulnerable people in the congregation? How intentional are they in showing hospitality?

Service: How are they serving at clubs or organised events – are they keen to be involved and helpful? When they participate, how do they engage with the team and community? Do they show initiative or wait to be told? Do they serve in any way in the local community?

Personal Relationships: How do they deal with confrontation with church members and members of the community? How do they interact and love the membership? Do they love well in practice and speech? Are they active members? What kind of questions do they ask at members' meetings?

For this activity, select the top three women who scored the most 5s and 4s. If she has multiple 5s, then work through her strongest point first. Prayerfully consider how best to use her gifts. She may be excellent at a lot of things, but are they things other people could do? What role, service or task do you think she can do that few others can?

| Name | |
|---|---|
| What gift(s) have you specifically seen? | |
| What actions have you specifically witnessed? | |
| How can you better use her gifts to serve the congregation? | |
| What is the role and the top three gifts needed? | |
| What's her starting point? | |
| What do you need to do to help her fulfil her role? | |

# APPENDIX 3:

# Guarding Your Heart Activity

How do I guard my heart and keep it tender towards God? This is a question we need to always keep in mind.

To enable us to guard our hearts in ministry we must be prepared to ask some hard questions of ourselves and invest our time in the right ways. I would suggest if we aren't getting the balance in our personal life right then that pattern will likely be seen in our ministry also.

I suggest you speak to your one-to-one and ask her to keep you accountable in the areas discussed below.

| Relationship to... | How am I doing in these areas? Score 1 to 9 (9 being the most satisfied). | What are my priorities? Score 1 to 9 how important each is to you (1 being the most important; use each number only once). |
|---|---|---|
| God | | |
| Finances | | |
| Family (Extended) | | |
| Self-Development | | |
| Marriage | | |
| Health | | |
| Hobbies | | |
| Children | | |
| Friendship | | |

List your top four priority relationships and describe what you want that relationship to look like:

1.

2.

3.

4.

## Read Colossians 3:1–15

1. What does the text say about God the Father and Christ?

2. What does the text say about mankind?

3. Form a small paragraph that sums up what you have just read.

Think about what you have written in your summary.

1. How would I be different if I was to take this and burn it into my inner being?

2. Why is God showing me this today? What is he saying to me specifically?

3. Does this truth impact how I think through my top four priorities?

## Top Four Priorities

Be honest: what is your current reality for these priority relationships? Think about what's getting in the way, the truth God has just highlighted, etc.

Priority 1.

Priority 2.

Priority 3.

Priority 4.

## Prayer and Action

1. Confess any sins that have been brought to mind.
2. Thank God for what has been revealed about his character, his grace and Christ.
3. Ask for God's help applying what you have learned today to your life and your top-four-priority list.

## How do things need to change? How are you going to get there?

Priority 1.

Priority 2.

Priority 3.

Priority 4.

There are times when we can't see the wood for the trees. It would be helpful to go through this document and discuss it with your one-to-one accountability person or someone who knows you really well and won't be afraid to be honest with you.

# APPENDIX 4:

# Passing on the DNA

## Activity 1: The Baseline Measurement

Think clearly about you want to see – at a minimum – happening in each of the following areas of women's ministry of your church or plant. If doing this in a group, come back together afterwards to discuss and provide feedback (you might even steal someone else's idea if it's good).

| Topic | The Baseline Standard |
|---|---|
| Evangelism | |
| Discipleship | |

| Accountability (one-to-one) | |
|---|---|
| Hospitality | |
| Service | |
| Care of the Membership (love in practice) | |
| Personal Relationship | |
| Other Topics Relevant to Your Congregation | |

## Activity 2: Do You Live Up to Your Own Standards?

Now is the hard part, as we are going to self-reflect. Don't do this with the wrong attitude. It's not about us finding out how rubbish we are and beating ourselves up. We aren't some sort of superwoman-style women's worker. There are several reasons for self-reflection:

1. Good reflection is always healthy and helpful. Through it, we can identify strengths and identify weaknesses that you may need further development in.

2. It may help you work through and identify gifts and skills that other women can supply.

3. It will help you think through the best way to 'pass the DNA on'. For example, maybe when it comes to teaching and development you need the help of others. Fontaine is particularly gifted in evangelism. You struggle in this area, so perhaps you should ask her to do a training session on it for your care team.

On the next page rank yourself in each topic below.

| Do you live up to your own standards? | Rank yourself 1 to 10 (10 being the highest) | Strength – how well are you doing in this? |
|---|---|---|
| Evangelism | | |
| Discipleship | | |
| Accountability (one-to-one) | | |
| Hospitality | | |
| Service | | |
| Care of the Membership (love in practice) | | |
| Personal Relationship | | |
| Other Topics Relevant to Your Congregation | | |

| Weakness – where are you struggling? | What positive changes can you make or help solicit from others? |
|---|---|
| | |
| | |
| | |
| | |
| | |
| | |
| | |
| | |

## How Can I Pass On the DNA?

Everyone is different. We learn and teach in different ways, and we must consider this when we think through how we can pass on the DNA.

Individual Approach: This is a one-to-one, mentoring and discipleship relationship. This is the most time-consuming relationship, but I think this produces the best results. We teach the DNA as we walk through life together. For someone who is more intuitive in the way they work, this is a great way to pass on DNA because you basically show them while they can observe and ask questions.

Small Group: In our experiences, six is a great number for a small group. Anything more than eight works less well. I have used the small-group method a lot. This is how we train the women in the care team at Niddrie and the women's workers for 20schemes. Think about it: we might be in a classroom, but the classes are small, which lends itself to prayer, interaction, questions, necessary pushback, mentoring opportunities and peer support. I can't tell you how important the one-anothering and mentoring that small group is. With a smaller group over a long period, you have a real opportunity for truthful individual interaction and evaluation at the same time. You get to see who is really getting it and applying it to their lives. For those who aren't, you may even get a hint in a small group as to what the barriers are to their learning.

Large Group Training: By this I mean sessions like our pre-conference and the sessions we have run at the Bible convention. There is definitely a place for this type of teaching, but it's detached and doesn't give as much room for flexibility, interaction and evaluation of application. Sometimes it feels like a drop in the ocean.

Resource and Book Method of Teaching: This approach is exactly what it sounds like. It is useful, but we need to be mindful not everyone learns this way.

## A Few Practical Pointers

1. Make a plan and identify what you need to teach and how to teach it.
2. Work out the training method and who can help you.
3. How will you honestly evaluate and review the training and the process?
4. Are you achieving your aims? Are you teaching the baseline, and is the DNA being passed on?

a division of 10 **of those**.com

10Publishing is the publishing house of 10ofThose.
It is committed to producing quality Christian
resources that are biblical and accessible.

www.10ofthose.com is our online retail arm selling
thousands of quality books at discounted prices.

For information contact: info@10ofthose.com
or check out our website: www.10ofthose.com